BOUQUET CHIC

BOUQUET CHIC

WEDDING FLOWERS FOR MORE THAN *160* ROMANTIC LOOKS

Kimberly Aurora Kapur

Photography by Jim Henkens

WATSON-GUPTILL PUBLICATIONS / NEW YORK

Published in the United States by Watson-Guptill
Publications, an imprint of the Crown Publishing Group,
a division of Random House, Inc., New York.
www.watsonguptill.com

ISBN-10: 0-8230-9181-3
ISBN-13: 978-0-8230-9181-2

Library of Congress Control Number: 2007942905

Watson-Guptill Publications books are available at special
discounts when purchased in bulk for premiums and sales
promotions, as well as for fundraising or educational use.
Special editions or book excerpts can be created.

Executive Editor: Joy Aquilino
Editor: Patricia Fogarty
Designer: Nita Ybarra
Production director: Alyn Evans

Photographer: Jim Henkens

Manufactured in Singapore

First printing, 2008

1 2 3 4 5 6 7 8 9 / 15 14 13 12 11 10 09 08

Acknowledgments

I WOULD FIRST LIKE TO THANK MY WONDERFUL HUSBAND, JAY, FOR YOUR FAITH and support. Special thanks to Jim Henkens, my photographer, for being on board from the very beginning and contributing your extraordinary talents. Many thanks to the following: my agent, Nancy Rosenthal, for her enthusiasm and for helping make this possible; my editors Joy Aquilino, for believing in this project, and Patricia Fogarty, for working to uncompromising standards. Thanks to Timothy Hsu and Nita Ybarra for their book design. I would also like to thank Scott Carlson, Michael Kimura, Chad Nelson, Ron Robertson, and Patrick Zweifel for their invaluable contributions of gorgeous flower product—you guys are the best! Thank you, Heidi Nymark, for your beautiful work on hair and makeup. I am thankful for everyone who had a hand in contributing to this book: Stacey Ahlgrim, Joni Boness, Blaise Bouchant, Courtney Capellan, Su Choi, Jodell Egbert, Kristen Elizabeth, Elizabeth Scott Frankenberg, Jennifer Gay, Mary Goodman, Meredith Griffin, Ruby Harnden, Kimberly Hoeshler (additional hair and makeup), Gina Isaacs, Klaudia Keller, Elizabeth Klove, Nicole Korman, Christine Liebsack, Amy Manne, Judy Mock, Holly Morris, Lindsay Nichols, Doug Otani, Aimee Page, Barb Penoyar, Simone Perry, Kristy Peterson, Kristy Ristine, Eric Rubles, Gretchen Scoebel, Madina Vadache, Luly Yang, and finally our models: Andreea Florescu, Erica Pederson, Adazoe Freeman, Evelia La Freniere, Anastasiya Mykaloust, and Morgan Reynolds—thanks for your great work! For playing a key role in my career in the wedding flower business, I am thankful for my parents, Nony and Debbie Capellan, and for Liisa Sewell, Kyoko Megurian, Erica Meisgeier, Karin Kuntz, and (in memory) Mark Wirth, who was greatly missed during this project. ❧

Contents

GWEN. *A bouquet of lace and roses was designed for a sensitive, romantic bride.* ♦♦

Preface

I BECAME A FLORIST MORE THROUGH KISMET THAN AMBITION. WHEN I WAS IN MY late teens, I saw that brides were drawn to wedding flowers done in a romantic style. Though I had worked as an assistant in flower shops starting at age fifteen, I had never been a designer. I was only nineteen and a college sophomore with a full course load when I made up business cards, took photographs of bridal bouquets I had made in my apartment, and sent them to a few local wedding coordinators. ❧ A few brides showed interest, and the following summer I had my first clients. That very fun summer job quickly grew into a full-time occupation—on top of my school work. I rented a studio on the east side of Seattle and soon was doing forty or more weddings a year. I later went national with RomanticFlowers.com, an online retail site for wedding decoration products. ❧ Through the years I have worked with hundreds of clients in Seattle and thousands of wonderful Web site customers around the country. Talking to women day in and day out has given me an acute sense of the dreams and desires of today's bride. Those dreams, which started my business and continue to fuel my efforts, are reflected in the bouquets in this book. My guiding philosophy is that I want my designs to reflect the bride's personal style and to help create a wedding she will always remember. ❧ With this book of bridal bouquets, I hope to convey not only my love for flowers, but also my interpretation of romance itself. I created these bouquets not just as unique floral designs but in service to an ideal: to represent a bride's heart—and her style—in a bouquet of flowers. I hope this book serves you well as an inspiring companion on your quest for the bridal bouquet of your dreams.

—Kimberly Aurora Kapur

HANNAH. *Beautiful, blushing flowers for the bride.* 12-inch hand-tied bouquet of coleus (summer–fall), tuberous begonias, peach hypericum, and blush mini calla lilies. Gown: Avioanni; veil: Cicada Bridal; necklace: Voletta Couture. ♦♦

Introduction

THE BRIDAL BOUQUET IS A VERY OLD SYMBOL WITH PAGAN ROOTS. IN ANCIENT Greece and Rome, brides carried bouquets, made of wheat or fragrant herbs, that symbolized fertility or were thought to ward off evil sprits. Over the centuries, the bouquet took on many other meanings. Today, bridal bouquets are fashioned from just about every flower under the sun and in a wide range of shapes and styles. ❧ The modern version of the bridal bouquet was popularized by England's Queen Victoria, who in 1840 carried a tussie-mussie (a tiny, round clutch of flowers in a filigree holder filled with moss) of orange blossoms; a coronet of orange blossoms trimmed her veil. Brides in the Victorian era carefully chose flowers for the sentiments they represented, and the blooms the bride carried were "her flowers" for the rest of her life. ❧ Modern brides may find the Victorian "language of flowers" charming, but its details have largely been forgotten. Yet the wedding bouquet remains symbolically significant, with a meaning not unlike what the Victorians imagined. It becomes an extension of the bride's personality and a symbol of her love. And no matter what types of flowers a bride chooses, the gathered blossoms she carries express her beauty, exuberance, love, and faithfulness.

THE LANGUAGE OF FLOWERS

In the early eighteenth century, Lady Mary Wortley Montagu, a writer and the wife of the British ambassador to Turkey, wrote letters from there describing the symbolism attached to various flowers in the East and detailing the message conveyed by each bloom. People in Europe and America, especially lovers, started using this "language of flowers" around the time of the French Revolution, sending flowers carefully chosen to convey particular sentiments. Since then, many books on the language of flowers (many with that very title) have been published.

Left: **KENZIE.** 10-inch hand-tied bouquet of 'Summer Fashion' garden roses, 'Vermeer' mini calla lilies, and dahlias (best summer–fall), trimmed with double-faced satin ribbon. Background flowers are dahlias, hydrangeas, and oriental lilies. The cost mainly reflects the price of its premium flowers, but it's a small bouquet and is easy to make because it's hand-tied. ♦♦♦

Right, top: **AMORA.** 14-inch hand-tied bouquet of 'Bluebird' roses, 'Pierre de Ronsard' roses, 'Mimi Eden' roses, dahlias (best summer–fall), 'Naked Lady' amaryllises (winter–spring), and dendrobium orchids. This bouquet has a lot of premium flowers but is fairly fast and easy to construct. ♦♦♦

Right, bottom: **KYLA.** In this 24-inch wired bouquet, hyacinths (late winter–spring), 'Bianca Candy' roses, dendrobium orchids, stephanotis, and mini tulle millenary flowers fall in a gorgeous cascade. This bouquet's high cost is due in part to large quantities of premium flowers, but the price mainly reflects labor costs—it takes about 6 hours to make. Roses, stephanotis, and tiny hyacinth blossoms all are removed from the stalk and individually wired, then wired into larger and larger clusters, and finally intricately wired in a balanced design. Most of the prep takes place just before the wedding, which drives up the costs. Only an experienced professional should attempt to make this bouquet. See page 129 for a larger photo. ♦♦♦♦♦♦

Introduction

THE BRIDAL BOUQUET IS A VERY OLD SYMBOL WITH PAGAN ROOTS. IN ANCIENT Greece and Rome, brides carried bouquets, made of wheat or fragrant herbs, that symbolized fertility or were thought to ward off evil sprits. Over the centuries, the bouquet took on many other meanings. Today, bridal bouquets are fashioned from just about every flower under the sun and in a wide range of shapes and styles. ❧ The modern version of the bridal bouquet was popularized by England's Queen Victoria, who in 1840 carried a tussie-mussie (a tiny, round clutch of flowers in a filigree holder filled with moss) of orange blossoms; a coronet of orange blossoms trimmed her veil. Brides in the Victorian era carefully chose flowers for the sentiments they represented, and the blooms the bride carried were "her flowers" for the rest of her life. ❧ Modern brides may find the Victorian "language of flowers" charming, but its details have largely been forgotten. Yet the wedding bouquet remains symbolically significant, with a meaning not unlike what the Victorians imagined. It becomes an extension of the bride's personality and a symbol of her love. And no matter what types of flowers a bride chooses, the gathered blossoms she carries express her beauty, exuberance, love, and faithfulness.

THE LANGUAGE OF FLOWERS

In the early eighteenth century, Lady Mary Wortley Montagu, a writer and the wife of the British ambassador to Turkey, wrote letters from there describing the symbolism attached to various flowers in the East and detailing the message conveyed by each bloom. People in Europe and America, especially lovers, started using this "language of flowers" around the time of the French Revolution, sending flowers carefully chosen to convey particular sentiments. Since then, many books on the language of flowers (many with that very title) have been published.

The Ultimate Accessory

Planning a look for her big day can feel like a daunting challenge for the bride-to-be. In the months leading up to the wedding, she slips into her dress for multiple fittings, practices doing her hair and makeup, and shops for the right shoes, veil, and jewelry. The bridal bouquet is often the last element to be considered—but it certainly should not be the least. The bouquet is the bride's ultimate accessory, her crowning glory as she walks down the aisle. How should she choose her bouquet flowers?

Some brides know just what they want. More typically, others consult with a floral designer. Even the savviest bride might not be familiar with the many flowers that are available, but most have an abstract image of their bouquet and can identify it when they see it. I use photos when I consult with a bride and carefully note her flower and style preferences. This book offers ideas to help brides and florists brainstorm.

My design process usually begins with inspiration from the dress, which reveals a lot about the bride's personal style. I ask for a photo of the dress (preferably of the bride wearing it) and a swatch of the material so I can see the color firsthand. Bridal fabrics can be a great source of inspiration.

I also ask about the makeup, jewelry, and hairstyles the bride is contemplating. Details like pearls in a veil or interesting jewelry can be useful cues. I consider how the bridesmaids' dresses might tie into the bridal bouquet, as well as where the ceremony will be held and its style and lighting. With these details in mind, I make suggestions for types of flowers and the color, line, texture, and shape of the bouquet. Then the bride and I discuss fun accent touches—ribbon ties, a tiny rhinestone brooch on the handle, a splash of unusual color—that add style and personality to a bridal bouquet.

DESIGN CONCEPTS

The cornerstone of my designs is the bride's style. For a sentimental bride, I may suggest how to match flowers to a lace dress. For a bride with traditional tastes who will wear an A-line ball gown, I might recommend a tight, formal dome bouquet. For me, bridal bouquet styles fall into four traditional categories. Each has its own chapter in this book—*something old:* classic, timeless concepts personalized for the contemporary bride; *something new:* designs, including sexy and exotic looks, that push the envelope of style or create modern classics; *something borrowed:* inspiration from family, friends, or the past, or designs that reinterpret vintage and heirloom ideas for today's bride; and *something blue:* designs that use special colors for a bride's flowers to accent her personality and style.

Today's fashion melds the old with the new, the borrowed with the blue (and other colors). I love juxtaposing the natural with the faux, the rich with the simple, the classic with the trendy. Most boutique florists are familiar with the flowers I use, and I aim to keep my ideas approachable while maintaining a flair for luxury and quality. My stylings are not for the sake of fashion. Rather, every bouquet is meant to enhance the bride's beauty in an elegant way.

CAPRICE. *Roses and gardenias are a good match for most bright, textured fabrics.* 10-inch hand-tied bouquet of 'Marie Claire' roses, gardenias (on wire stems), and sweet peas (spring–early summer). ♦♦♦

Left: **KENZIE.** 10-inch hand-tied bouquet of 'Summer Fashion' garden roses, 'Vermeer' mini calla lilies, and dahlias (best summer–fall), trimmed with double-faced satin ribbon. Background flowers are dahlias, hydrangeas, and oriental lilies. The cost mainly reflects the price of its premium flowers, but it's a small bouquet and is easy to make because it's hand-tied. ♦♦♦

Right, top: **AMORA.** 14-inch hand-tied bouquet of 'Bluebird' roses, 'Pierre de Ronsard' roses, 'Mimi Eden' roses, dahlias (best summer–fall), 'Naked Lady' amaryllises (winter–spring), and dendrobium orchids. This bouquet has a lot of premium flowers but is fairly fast and easy to construct. ♦♦♦

Right, bottom: **KYLA.** In this 24-inch wired bouquet, hyacinths (late winter–spring), 'Bianca Candy' roses, dendrobium orchids, stephanotis, and mini tulle millenary flowers fall in a gorgeous cascade. This bouquet's high cost is due in part to large quantities of premium flowers, but the price mainly reflects labor costs—it takes about 6 hours to make. Roses, stephanotis, and tiny hyacinth blossoms all are removed from the stalk and individually wired, then wired into larger and larger clusters, and finally intricately wired in a balanced design. Most of the prep takes place just before the wedding, which drives up the costs. Only an experienced professional should attempt to make this bouquet. See page 129 for a larger photo. ♦♦♦♦♦♦

Bouquet Key

THE BOUQUETS THAT appear in the chapters that follow are described
in captions giving the following information:

BOUQUET SIZE. Unless otherwise noted, the size noted in the caption is the bouquet's diameter.

FLOWERS. Each flower species has at least two names: a common name (lily-of-the-valley) and a Latinized scientific name (*Convallaria majalis*) that combines a capitalized genus name and a species name. Flowers can have many common names, but each has only one scientific name, which allows it to be identified anywhere around the world. The captions use the most popular common names for flowers. Species sometimes have "nicknames," identified with double quotation marks, and within some species there are cultivated varieties, identified by names within single quotation marks. I give the names of varieties of roses and the genus names for orchids, but most other flowers are not well known by variety or genus, so I simply give the common name. The Flower Names section that begins on page 154 gives the scientific names for the flowers identified by common name throughout the book.

METHOD OF CONSTRUCTION. Most bouquets in this book are either hand-tied or wired; the caption notes the method used. See Chapter 1 for details on how to construct hand-tied and wired bouquets.

COST. The cost of each bouquet is estimated in six categories—indicated by diamonds that appear following the caption—based on a combination of the price of the flowers, accessory materials, and labor.

A bouquet with one diamond uses inexpensive materials and is easy to construct. Six diamonds means that the bouquet requires many hours of construction (by you or a florist) and/or uses a large quantity of expensive flowers and/or materials.

AVAILABILITY. Each flower has a natural blooming season, but seasonality does not always determine when it may be available on the cut-flower market. Many varieties are grown out of their natural season in hothouses or are imported from other climates. Imported and hothouse flowers can be more expensive than local field flowers, but if there is abundant supply their prices can be more reasonable, even comparable to locally grown flowers. That said, I like to stick with flower varieties that are not impossible for a florist to source. For those who want to create a bouquet described here when the recommended flowers are out of season, I suggest substitutions. And even if you choose a flower that is widely available year-round, it's wise to have a back-up choice; the market is not perfect, even for the most resourceful florist. In the captions for each bouquet in the chapters that follow, limitations in the typical availability of a flower are given in parentheses following the flower name; seasons noted are when the flower is most available, though your florist may still be able to find it for you beyond those times. When a note about availability does not appear, the flower should be available throughout the year.

ALLEGRA. *A designer bouquet to match a signature piece of jewelry.* 12-inch hand-tied bouquet of yellow spray roses, 'Super Green' roses, black kale, purple kale, 'Blue Curiosa' roses, and 'Mimi Eden' spray roses. Gown: Madina Vadache; necklace: Michal Negrin. ♦♦♦♦

1
Bouquet Essentials

I'VE DESIGNED THIS BOOK TO SERVE TWO PURPOSES. IF YOU ARE LOOKING FOR ideas but don't plan to construct the bouquet yourself, the book will help you to fall in love with great flower combinations and to develop a designer's eye. Plus, it will give you the basic information to talk knowledgeably with florists and to select the right bouquet. If you want to make your own bouquet, it provides details about materials and techniques. ❧ Planning to do your own flowers? Confidence is the key, and it comes from having a strong sense of style and some know-how. Another essential word of advice: Practice. Between now and your wedding, get your hands on as many flowers as you can—from your garden, florist, or grocer—and make mock-up bouquets. You don't have to use the flowers you've chosen for the big day, but you do need to accustom your hands to working easily with flowers. ❧ The good news is that simple techniques can result in a lush look. Many of the bouquets in this book look rich and opulent, but the techniques for making them are easy and straightforward. I use hand-tying—one of the easiest ways to make flower arrangement—most often when designing bridal bouquets. Wiring flowers is more time-consuming and requires lots of practice. A good professional florist needs to have mastered both skills. ❧ Apart from the techniques of hand-tying and wiring, most floral design is in the creative details—deciding on the right color combinations, mixing sizes and textures, fashioning unique shapes, and adding fun ribbons and other accessories. Creativity can't really be taught, but hopefully I can put you on a path toward it with a healthy dose of inspiration!

Bouquet Shapes

The best shape for a bridal bouquet is one that matches the silhouette of the bride's gown and that complements her frame. The classic round bouquet can be designed in many variations. A cascading bouquet creates drama. An arm-held bouquet can be seen from all sides. And any bouquet shape can be sized to suit the bride's proportions.

Dome

Posy

Nosegay

Natural bouquet

Concentric bouquet

Formal spray

Bouquet in an armature

Abstract spray

ROUND BOUQUETS

Nosegay. This term for a small grouping of flowers traditionally refers to scented flowers in a tiny clutch bouquet, but it has come to mean any type of flower in a small, round bouquet. In Victorian times, a nosegay with flowers and herbs chosen according to the "language of flowers" (see Introduction) was called a tussie-mussie. **Dome.** A tightly arranged bouquet in a hemisphere shape is called a dome. **Natural bouquet.** The overall shape is round or domed, but some of the flowers may be arranged off-plane from the spherical shape to give the bouquet a looser look. **Formal spray.** The flowers are arranged loosely and radiate symmetrically from the center. **Abstract spray.** Flowers radiate outward in a relaxed, asymmetrical fashion. **Posy.** This word, another term for "bouquet," usually connotes a diminutive one, often with a "just picked" look and with stems exposed. **Concentric bouquet.** Concentric circles of like flowers are the basis of this bouquet. Concentric arrangements are sometimes called Biedermeier bouquets. **Bouquet in an armature.** A framework of branches or greenery is used to hold the flowers in place, as though the bouquet is a nest in a tree. The framework often is abstract and features crisscrossed lines.

CASCADE BOUQUETS

Garland. Wired flowers are wrapped and taped on a garland rope (available at florist supply stores), and a wire handle is attached at the end of the garland. This bouquet is held at the hip or side. **Teardrop cascade.** A short cascade is often called a teardrop. **Asymmetrical or crescent cascade.** These types of cascade bouquets have a "tail" off to the side. A crescent has a tail on two sides, giving the bouquet a half-moon shape. An asymmetrical cascade tails off to one side, as shown. **Spray arm cascade.** This loose spray of flowers, complemented by trailing greenery, weeping flowers, or strung flower garlands, is held on the forearm. **Cathedral cascade.** This long, flowing cascade can be shaped in a strict symmetrical shape or in a loose form, as shown.

Asymmetrical or crescent cascade

Garland

Cathedral cascade

Spray arm cascade

Teardrop cascade

Arm spray

Presentation bouquet

ARM BOUQUETS

Presentation bouquet. This long-stemmed arm bouquet is carried on the forearm like a wand or scepter. **Arm spray.** Held on the forearm and supported by the opposite hand, the spray may cascade downward and over the arm.

Conditioning Flowers

It is very important to purchase flowers from a quality source (see page 21). Buy flowers that are free of rot, discoloration, bruising, and breakage, and that are not too tight or too open. Every flower requires unique care, but generally flowers should be kept out of drafts and direct sun, and away from sources of ethylene, such as fruit, car exhaust, and trash. Keep vases and buckets clean, and use a commercial floral preservative. Delicate flowers, such as stephanotis or gardenias, last only a day out of refrigeration, but some tropicals can last as long as several weeks. Most garden flowers and roses will last five to ten days at room temperature. Keep flowers cool until the day of the wedding; many flowers like to be misted with cool water. Here are a few tips about how to care for some of the most popular wedding flowers and related materials:

ROSES. Store roses in a tall bucket to keep the stems upright; if roses are stored in a short vase and rest at an angle, the weight of the heads can cause them to droop. Don't remove the thorns until just before the bouquet is constructed, to prevent bacteria from entering the stems and harming the flowers. Metal thorn strippers can damage the flesh of the stem, so I wear pigskin gloves to remove the foliage and leave the thorns intact until just before constructing the bouquet. The optimal storage temperature is 38–40 degrees Fahrenheit, but roses can be stored at room temperature for several days before the wedding to allow them to open properly. They open much more slowly when they are stored in a refrigerator.

TULIPS. Place tulips in cold water and keep them in the dark, at 34 degrees Fahrenheit. Keep closed tulips out of the light until just before the wedding. If you want them to look floppy or open, store them out of the cooler the night before the wedding.

SAPPY FLOWERS. Flowers with sappy stems—like daffodils or euphorbia—contain irritants that will harm other flowers. Add them to the bouquet just before you wrap the stem. To prevent the stems from dripping sap, singe the stem bottom with a flame.

HYDRANGEAS. Humidity (constant misting) is crucial to keeping hydrangea blossoms happy. An easier method is to lay a wet paper towel directly on the blossoms while they are stored (at 40 degrees Fahrenheit) or to cover the flower heads loosely with a plastic bag; lift off the plastic every few hours and mist the blooms heavily. Wilting, which can occur with hydrangeas, is best prevented by dipping newly cut stems in boiling water for 30 seconds and then immediately transferring them to lukewarm water.

LILIES. Place tulips in cold water and keep them in the dark, at 34 degrees Fahrenheit. Keep closed tulips out of the light until just before the wedding. If you want them to look floppy or open, store them out of the cooler the night before the wedding.

ORCHIDS. Orchids should be stored at 55 degrees Fahrenheit, so in temperate climates it is not always necessary to use a cooler. Orchids are very delicate—their petals are susceptible to breaking and bruising from even a small impact. Be very careful when placing orchids on a table. I often wrap orchid bouquets with cotton batting when I'm storing and delivering them.

CALLA LILIES. Because these flowers are susceptible to stem rot, invert the stems and fill their spongy cavities with water. Keep them in about 2 inches of water that's about 50 degrees Fahrenheit. Taping the stems together and storing them in a dark vase can help keep them from bending. When you take the stems out of the water, let them dry for about 30 minutes before the bride will carry the bouquet.

GREENERY. Store greenery in about 2 inches of water. Change the water daily, since some of the leaves will still be underwater, which causes a buildup of bacteria that smells bad and will shorten the vase life of the greenery.

PREMIUM FLOWER HEADS. Stephanotis, gardenias, and some orchids are sold by the head, without stems. They should be stored in a cooler, ideally a commercial one, at 40 degrees Fahrenheit and with high humidity. If these flower heads are to be stored in a food refrigerator, wrap them in plastic.

HOLLOW STEMS. Turn delphiniums, dahlias, and amaryllis upside down and fill their stems with cold water. Plug the stems with cotton, quickly turn them right side up, and place them in a bucket of fresh lukewarm water.

CUTTING YOUR OWN GARDEN FLOWERS. Cut garden flowers just before they open or when they are only partially open. After cutting, give them at least two hours—preferably a full day—to open before you arrange them. Cut flowers early in the morning, and avoid cutting them in the afternoon sun.

MIA. *Tiny details, such as crystal inserts, can make a simple bouquet a small masterpiece.* This 10-inch wired bouquet brings together 'Sweet Akito' roses, cymbidium orchids, sweet peas (spring–early summer), and stephanotis. ♦♦♦♦

Buy Flowers from a Quality Source

Relying on reputation is important. Professional florists are familar with wholesalers and growers, but if you are an individual buying directly from a florist on the retail level or on the Internet, be sure to ask friends, family members, or a wedding coordinator for recommendations of florists to buy from or those to avoid. If you plan to purchase flowers on the Internet, talk or establish e-mail contact with someone at the company and have your concerns answered before you buy. You may want to place a sample order before committing to a larger purchase. Whatever your source, establish a relationship with someone who will be accountable for the prompt delivery and the quality of your order.

Assembling a Bouquet: Two Techniques

The two main techniques employed for most bouquets are hand-tying and wiring. Hand-tying is an easy method of gathering loose flowers on their natural stems, binding them together with wire and tape, and finishing off the arrangement with ribbon or another wrap.

If the stems are too short to hand-tie or if you want to create a wide variety of shapes that cannot be achieved with stems, you may choose to use wiring—an advanced method for creating a wide variety of bouquet shapes. Wiring involves removing the stem altogether and replacing it with a wire, then taping over the wire to finish it off. Wired stems can be taped together in clusters to form a bouquet.

It can be useful to mix the two methods. I often wire individual blossoms on long wires and then assemble them in hand-tying bouquets. I stick with the two traditional techniques of hand-tied and wiring in most cases. I use floral foam bases for bridal bouquets only occasionally—for example, for a loose spray of very lightweight flowers (sweet peas or pansies, or a lightweight vine like clematis) that need constant hydration.

Tools of the trade: Basic.
You will need these tools to make a hand-tied bouquet.

Binding wire

Waterproof tape

Utility knife

Pinking shears

The Hand-Tied Bouquet

A hand-tied bouquet, suitable for all types of stemmed flowers, is simple and less expensive to make than a wired bouquet. It is the method I recommend if you have little or no experience working with flowers but want to make your own bouquet. Hand-tying takes little prep and design time, and flowers on their stems are much easier to care for than delicate, wired bouquets. Hand-tied bouquets, which can be made with a thick stem handle that exposes the bottom of the stems beneath the ribbon wrap, also have a unique, "just-picked" look. Foliage on the stems can also be retained for a natural backdrop to the flowers. Hand-tying is especially suitable for creating bouquets in round shapes, from loose sprays to tight nosegays. For outdoor ceremonies, hand-tied bouquets have an advantage in that they withstand sun and intense heat better than wired bouquets.

MAKING A HAND-TIED BOUQUET

Step 1. Using a utility knife, remove foliage up to the gathering point of the bouquet. Hold the flower with the head toward you and run the knife down the stem to remove unwanted leaves. The more foliage that remains on the flowers, the looser the bouquet will be. When working with roses, I leave the thorns intact and wear pigskin gloves for protection as I remove the foliage.

Step 2. Gather the stems together, adding them one by one at an angle, turning the bouquet as you go. Place the heads of the flowers at different levels or keep them on one plane.

Step 3. Bind the stems just below the blossoms with waterproof tape or binding wire.

Step 4. If you are working with roses, remove the thorns by hand (metal thorn strippers can damage the stem). You can do this as part of Step 1, if you like, but don't remove the thorns until you're ready to assemble the bouquet.

Step 5. Bind the stems together near the bottom, and cut with a sharp pruner (also called a secatur).

Voilà! Beautiful! See page 32 for how to do a basic spiral ribbon wrap.

THE WIRED BOUQUET

Flowers are wired to reduce the bulk of natural stems or to provide a substitute "stem" when flower heads have short stems or have been removed from their natural stem or vine.

Wiring a bouquet has two advantages: It reduces the weight and bulk of the stems, and allows you to create dramatic shapes. Wiring also lets you design with flowers that have short stems or with florets that have no stems (such as gladioli removed from their large stems). With wired flowers you can create cascades, teardrops, crescents, and many other interesting shapes, yet wired bouquets can be very tight or fairly loose.

It takes experience to master wiring flowers, and this method generally should be left to a professional. The labor involved in wiring adds to the cost of your bouquet—an important consideration if you are on a budget. If you are a beginner who wants to master this skill for your wedding, I suggest that you regularly practice wiring flowers.

Wired bouquets are very delicate and must be refrigerated immediately after creation and up to the time when the bride will carry them. Many wired flowers are very short-lived, and in general they are more sensitive to the rigors (light and heat) of an outdoor ceremony, though there are exceptions to this rule—orchids and many other tropical flowers hold up well on wires.

When a flower is wired, florist tape (stretchy tape that sticks to itself as it is pulled taut around the wire) is used to cover the wire.

Tools of the trade: Master. If you plan to make a wired bouquet, you will need additional "master tools." The weight, or gauge, of the wire determines its strength: the lower the gauge number, the stronger the wire. Choose a gauge that will support the flower head. The right gauge is one that, once the wire is taped, allows you to slightly bend the wire at the neck without the head flopping over. For large roses, I use #22 gauge wire, and for small sweetheart roses, #26 gauge.

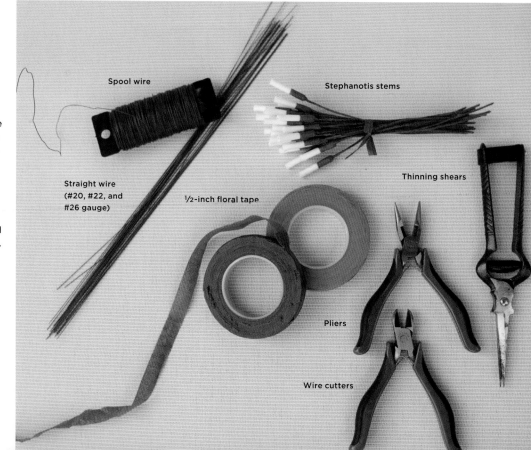

Spool wire

Stephanotis stems

Thinning shears

Straight wire (#20, #22, and #26 gauge)

½-inch floral tape

Pliers

Wire cutters

Tulip

Rose

Dendrobium orchid

Phalaenopsis orchid

Gladiolus

Which flowers to wire?

Any type of flower can be wired. Roses and orchids hold up very well to wiring. Although tulips are beautiful on their natural stems, I might wire them to create a tight nosegay or a cascade style; because their stems can bend in the light, it is easier to control the bouquet shape if they are wired. Other flowers, like gladioli, have large, stalky stems. I love the wide range of gladiolus colors, so I pluck the individual blossoms off the stalk and wire them.

How to wire a single rose blossom.

If the stem remains on the rose you will wire, remove most of it with sharp thinning shears and run two wires crosswise and at right angles, as shown, through the calyx (the flower head's bulbous base). Bend the wires down and then tape them together.

How to tape wire "stems."

Wrap the calyx with floral tape and hold the flower with one hand. With the opposite hand, pull the tape downward to stretch it, then twist or twirl the flower with your fingertips to wrap the wire "stem." Pull down, twisting, until you reach the end of the wire. The tape sticks to itself, so it just needs to be cut off at the end.

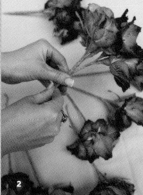

MAKING A WIRED BOUQUET

Step 1. To make a 10-inch bouquet, start with 40 stems of medium-size flowers (here I used 25 'Gypsy Curiosa' roses and 15 gladioli). Wire roses as described in "How to wire a single rose blossom," on page 25. For gladioli, use a very light wire and run the wires through the base of the floret, where the petals start.

Step 2. Gather 3 taped flowers (2 roses and 1 gladiolus) at a time and tape them together in small clusters.

Step 3. Tape together 3 of the small clusters from Step 2 to make a large cluster of 9 flowers. Repeat Steps 2 and 3 until you have 3 large clusters.

Step 4. Tape the 3 clusters together. Add the 13 extra flowers to fill in the shape of the bouquet. Gently bend the wired "stems" of the flowers apart so that the bouquet is not too tight. Even out the bottom of the "handle" by cutting off any excess with wire cutters.

Voilà! Spiral-wrap the stems with ribbon (see pages 32 and 33), secure it with a corsage pin, and you have a gorgeous bouquet.

MAKING A COMB OF FLOWERS

Fresh-plucked garden flowers can look beautiful in the bride's hair. They hold best when they are wired to a comb.

Step 1. Wire and tape a 'Tenga Venga' rose, and cut the wire to about a 1-inch "stem." Tape a 12-inch piece of wire and begin wrapping it through the teeth of the 2-inch comb and over the wired rose, laid lengthwise along the top crosspiece of the comb.

Step 2. Continue to add wired roses as you wind the taped wire through the comb's teeth and around the crosspiece.

Step 3. When you reach the end of the crosspiece, wrap the wire in the reverse direction, adding roses facing the opposite direction as you go. To secure the wire, wind it several times tightly in one place, then use pliers to twist the end as you connect it to the starting piece of wire. Cut off any excess wire. Insert the comb into the hair near the nape of the neck and secure it with hairpins.

MAKING A CASCADING GARLAND

There are two ways to make a cascading garland: stringing flowers and wiring them around a garland string. For the first method, simply run a long strand of light-gauge wire or a needle and a length of waxed string through individual blossoms, as if you were stringing beads. This method works best with uniform flowers, like the stephanotis blossoms shown here. Orchids are another popular choice (see Amora, page 14). Then incorporate the strung flowers into a wired bouquet; here the cascading stephanotis tendrils set off a dome of wired roses. A trailing garland is simple and elegant.

Or make a single large garland as a bouquet (see Bonita, page 147), though this is an advanced technique that perhaps only someone experienced in working with flowers should attempt. Wire and tape individual blooms (see page 25), then tape small clusters of the flowers around a garland rope (available at floral and craft supply shops) that forms the center of the design. The result will look like a long corsage. At the end of the garland, I bend a couple of heavy-gauge wires and tape them into the design to form a handle.

Right: **KATHERINE.** In this classic bouquet, stephanotis strung on wax twine creates a long, trailing effect. See it carried by a bride wearing an elegant, understated ensemble on page 59.

Accessorizing with Luxurious Ribbons and Other Accents

Ribbons and other accessories take a bouquet from plain and simple to a design masterpiece. Ribbons provide an extra dimension of color, texture, and luxury and are a great way to link your flowers and your dress. Not many flowers are blue, so I often use a blue ribbon, which looks great with any color of bouquet. And ribbons in funky, contrasting colors can be striking. Favorite ribbons for weddings include pure silks, shiny double-faced satins, preppie grosgrains, sumptuous jacquards, romantic taffetas, prim viscose, and luscious velvets. When working with the ribbon techniques described on page 31, use a thread that matches the color of the ribbon. Topstitch quality thread is usually best.

I also like to wire shells, pinecones, and other items from nature, as well as buttons, post-mounted jewels, glass-headed pins, and beaded ornaments that can be mounted on wires and secured with a few twists with pliers (tape over unfinished wires). For buttons, beads, and bows use a fabric-coated wire that does not need taping. Mount small seashells on chenille-coated wire; add a dab of superglue on the end of a wire and insert it inside a hollow shell (see the marginellas in the "Dress up your bouquet" photo). Bouquet baubles, such as Swarovski crystal beads or spray pearls, are sold mounted on long-stemmed posts.

YVETTE. *Bows on wires—each with a tiny crystal bead in the center—make a lovely, soft framework for this bouquet.* 8-inch wired bouquet of cymbidium orchids and stephanotis clusters, trimmed with 1-inch double-faced seafoam satin ribbon and crystal beads. ♦ ♦ ♦

Ribbon types.
You can wrap the stems of your bouquet with many different types of ribbon. Choose a ribbon for its color, style, and texture.

Rayon trim

Grosgrain

Dupioni silk

Dot viscose

Hand-dyed silk

Viscose

Silk double-faced satin

Velvet

Organdy

Chiffon ombre

Moiré taffeta

Wired taffeta

Dress up your bouquet.
Use one or more of these fun and stylish bouquet trims or inserts.

Shells (marginellas) glued on chenille wires

Duponi silk ribbon

Wired lichen

Vintage button

Wired pinecones

Beaded flower

Jewel mounted on post

Bullion wire

Satin bow on wire with a Swarovski crystal bead

Spray pearls

Glass-headed pins

Extra fancy bouquets. WHAT ACCESSORIZING CAN DO.

Top: **CARMEN.** Cymbidium orchids, honey-colored hypericum, and dusty miller. ♦♦♦

Left: **KAYDECE.** Cymbidium orchids, sweet peas (spring–early summer), hyacinths (late winter–spring), and 'Super Green' roses. ♦♦♦

Right: **ALLEGRA.** Yellow spray roses, 'Super Green' roses, black kale, purple kale, 'Blue Curiosa' roses, and 'Mimi Eden' spray roses. ♦♦♦♦

Yarn wrap

Layered, ruffled ribbons with appliqué

Appliquéd ribbon, simply wrapped

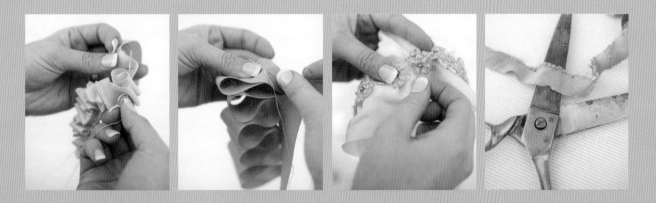

Crinkling ribbon. Run thread through the ribbon randomly as you crinkle it. After a few inches, secure your work by taking a stitch three times in the same spot. Repeat. For a finished example, see "Malia" on page 80.

Making "ribbon candy" ribbon. Fold 2-inch grosgrain ribbon over about every 2 inches. Secure the folds in place by stitching in the same spot three times, then cut the thread. Repeat. For a finished example, see "Phoebe" on page 99.

Attaching appliqué. Choose a thread close to the color of the appliqué. Every few inches, secure the appliqué, stitching in the same spot three times, then cut the thread. For a finished example, see the "Extra Fancy Bouquets" photo on page 30.

Distressing a silk ribbon. Create an "antiqued" effect on ribbons with a raw edge (such as silk dupioni, shown) by holding the edge of the ribbon taut over a scissors blade and pulling the length of the ribbon along the blade. Distress just one edge or both edges.

Pleating a ribbon. Pin the ribbon in place and run a stitch down the center. I love using this technique with taffetas. For an example on a finished bouquet, see "Amanda" on pages 114 and 115.

Ruffling or ruching a ribbon. To create a ruffled effect, use a sewing machine and run thread through the center of the length of the ribbon, gathering it gently into little tucks as you go. Or do it by hand: Pass a needle and thread in a straight line above and below the ribbon's surface, then pull the thread to create a gently gathered effect; if needed, tack each little tuck in place with a needle and thread. The result

will be a "ruffled" look that adds a frilly touch. This is a great technique for most ribbon types, including sheers. Be sure to use a matching thread. A nice, shiny topstitch thread looks good on satins, and an all-purpose, silky polyester works well with sheer organdies or taffetas. For a finished example, see "Blythe" on page 45.

Layering ruffles. For this technique, use two types of ribbon, one on top of the other, and ruffle the top layer as you sew. Use a bobbin thread that is the same color as the ribbon on the bottom layer. For an example, see "Katelyn" on pages 36 and 39.

THE BASIC SPIRAL RIBBON WRAP

Most hand-tied and wired bouquet stems can be wrapped with a simple spiral wrap.

Step 1. Starting near the stem ends, insert a pin through the end of the ribbon and into the stems. For a fresh-picked look on a hand-tied bouquet, leave some of the stems partially exposed.

Step 2. Pull the ribbon around the stem, spiraling upward and overlapping the ribbon substantially and evenly.

Step 3. Cut the end of the ribbon with pinking shears for a non-fraying finish, and insert corsage pins to secure. You will encounter less resistance if you angle the inserted pins upward, in the direction the wires or stems run. For a designer touch, insert several pins along the ribbon wrap.

Right: **SHERIDAN.** *Leathery-looking bergenia leaves are a rich mahogany color.* 10-inch hand-tied bouquet of mini calla lilies, "Siam Tulip" curcuma, parrot tulips (spring), and bergenia leaves, trimmed with ⅝-inch grosgrain ribbon that has a stitching pattern on the edges; the pins are metallic pink corsage pins. ♦♦

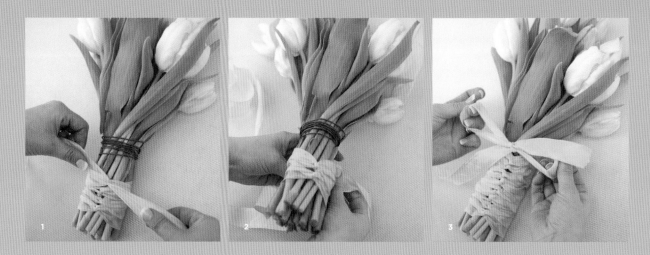

THE FRENCH BRAID WRAP

The French braid wrap is a step up from a basic spiral ribbon wrap and is an easy way to add a touch of style to your bouquet.

Step 1. In this example, I wrapped a simple hand-tied bouquet of white tulips. Start with 5 to 8 yards of ribbon (wrap the length around the bouquet first to make sure you have enough before cutting). Use ribbon that is ⅝-inch to 2 inches wide. (Here I used 5 yards of ⅞-inch wired taffeta.) Wrap the stem starting at the bottom of the bouquet. As you bring the two ends of the ribbon to the front, crisscross the ribbon, alternately switching the ends to the other hand.

Step 2. Bring the ribbon around the back after each cross in the front, keeping the left side under the right side. Repeat as you move up the stem. Slide the ribbon down the stem as you work so that the braids are closer together.

Step 3. Finish by tying a knot, then a bow over the knot. You can spiral-wrap the stem first with one color and then overwrap the ribbon with the French braid technique using a ribbon of a different color; make widely spaced braids and let the bottom layer show through for a pretty contrast look.

THE PETAL RIBBON STEM WRAP

This very simple wrap technique provides dramatic results. Start with about 5 yards of unwired double-faced satin, silk, viscose, or taffeta ribbon that is 2 to 3 inches wide. For this bouquet of peonies and ranunculus, I used 2½-inch viscose ribbon. Ruche the ribbon using a sewing machine (see instructions on page 31).

Step 1. Use a pearl pin to secure the end of the ribbon into the stems. Begin wrapping the bouquet stem from the top.

Step 2. As you wrap the ribbon around the stems, insert a few pins into the stitching you've done to create the ruching. Overlap the ribbon to keep the lines of stitching fairly close together.

Step 3. Secure the end of the ribbon with a pearl pin through the central stitching. Fluff out the ribbon to create a gorgeous "petal" effect.

1

2

3

Voilà! A beautiful finished product. You can either leave an inch or so of the stems exposed or wrap them to the bottom. If you don't want to hold a bulky thickness of stems, use this technique on a wired bouquet; its gathered "stems" tend to be more slender than those of a hand-tied bouquet. See "Dulce" on page 74 for another photo of this bouquet.

33

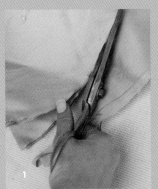

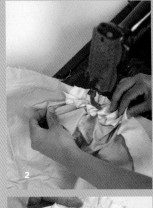

MACHIKO. *A beautiful sleeve protects and frames delicate, scented blooms.* 9-inch hand-tied bouquet of double 'Erlicheer' paperwhite narcissus (late winter–spring). ♦♦♦

MAKING A BOUQUET SLEEVE

The sleeve is made from ¼ yard of dupioni silk fabric, 1½ yards of 2-inch dupioni silk ribbon, and 1 yard of decorative trim.

Step 1. To create a 30-inch diameter circle from the dupioni silk fabric, fold the fabric twice and cut a 15-inch radius quarter circle on the bias.

Step 2. Layer and ruche both the circle and the length of 2-inch dupioni silk ribbon through the sewing machine. Layer appliqué over the seam. Distress the edges of the ribbon and silk with scissors. (See page 31 for instructions on layering, ruching, appliquéing, and distressing.)

Step 3. When the circle has been ruched, it will be shaped like a pouch. Insert the paperwhite bouquet into the pouch.

Step 4. Cinch at the top of the stems, and tie a silk ribbon around the base to secure the bouquet within the sleeve.

Preparing a bouquet to travel. Mist a finished bouquet with fresh water and lay it on a bed of tissue or shredded paper. To keep the flowers from becoming parched, cover the bouquet loosely with plastic and keep it out of sun and heat. In summer, to protect bouquets and keep them cool, I deliver them in a Styrofoam cooler box lined with shredded paper and ice packs. Don't let the flowers sit on the ice directly. Keeping the bouquet in a box with ice is essential for the most delicate wired bouquets, such as those with stephanotis or gardenias. Hand-tied bouquets can be kept in water; however, don't wrap the stems with ribbon until the bouquet is out of water and the stems have been dried.

KATELYN. *A bride floats on a sea of fabric and floral ruffles.* 12-inch wired bouquet of cattleya orchids, daffodils (late winter–spring), paperwhite narcissus (late winter–spring), and stephanotis. Double-faced satin ribbon is adorned with applied silk ribbon ruffle. Gown: Madina Vadache. ♦♦♦♦

2

Something Old: Classic Wedding Style

IT CAN BE EXCITING TO THINK ABOUT INCORPORATING FASHION TRENDS AS YOU plan your wedding bouquet. But like the bride who plans to wear a contemporary sheath and then is swept away by the loveliness of a frilly "princess" ball gown, you may find that you want to revisit such classics as a spray of wired gardenias or a clutch of lily-of-the-valley. I love to match flowers to gowns that incorporate the classic fashion elements of lace, ruffles, jewels, and bows. ❧ Flowers gain and lose favor as fashion trends shift and new generations of brides come to prefer various colors, forms, and scents. However, as attitudes change, some things— the popularity of the rose, the elegance of a white, scented bouquet—remain constant. When I plan a classic bouquet, I am inspired by nostalgia for the sweet pea, the enduring popularity of the tulip, and our lasting romance with the orchid. ❧ In this section I capture the essence of traditional bridal flowers and fashion them anew.

A BRIEF HISTORY OF CHANGING FLORAL STYLES

In the nineteenth and early twentieth centuries, brides preferred flowers with pleasing aromas and delicate forms that represented the "feminine" traits of fragility, sweetness, purity, and humility. Victorian and Edwardian flowers—sweet peas, violets, orange blossoms, forget-me-nots, carnations, lily-of-the-valley—became wedding classics.

In the early twentieth century, Asian influences helped inspire the Art Nouveau and Art Deco movements and popularized lilies and giant calla lilies. When movie stars wore gardenias and cattleya orchids, the demand for them soared. Transcontinental shipping and refrigerated trucking opened the market for exotic flowers.

In the mid-twentieth century, brides tended to favor large flowers and bright colors, choosing gladioli, carnations, and chrysanthemums for their size and novelty. Bouquets included lace and feathers; some brides even carried bouquets in fun shapes, such as a heart or a kissing ball. Others chose a decorated fan, a candle, or a prayer book in place of a bouquet.

As greenhouse technologies and international shipping expanded toward the end of the twentieth century, brides could have the flowers they wanted, regardless of season. Many chose bold and romantic garden-style flowers, such as hydrangeas, even in winter and spring.

Luxurious Touches

Modern wedding gowns can be spectacularly detailed. Some of the more popular touches are classic feminine elements such as ruffles, lace, and pretty bows. They help inspire me as I dream up couture touches to add to the bouquet design.

RUFFLES

I love designing bouquets for ruffled dresses. You can use just about any flowers with a ruffled feminine dress, but I like the challenge of finding ruffles in flowers, such as the center of a daffodil or the petals of a cattleya orchid. In spring, I mix columbine with daffodils and sweet peas—the texture of these flowers is crisp and their shape is curvilinear, making them a perfect match. In summer, I like gloriosa lilies and bougainvillea for their ruffled, waxy petals, which look tropical and delicate. In fall and winter, I might use kale rosettes mixed with purple cattleya orchids.

Left: **AVIVA.** *Very easy to make.* 10-inch bouquet of sweet peas (spring–early summer) and ruffled pansies (spring–fall, but best in spring) in a floral foam–filled metallic holder, to keep the delicate, short-stemmed pansies constantly hydrated. Buy foam pre-molded into a holder at a florist or floral craft-supply store. ♦♦

Right: **MIMI.** *Diminutive 'La Parisienne' roses have sweet, round faces and slightly ruffled petals.* 10-inch hand-tied bouquet of 'La Parisienne' roses, trimmed with 2 1/2-inch ruffle-edge satin ribbon. ♦♦♦

KATELYN. (also shown on page 36) In spring and early summer, instead of costly cattleya orchids, mix white sweet peas with yellow daffodils. In summer and fall, substitute garden roses for daffodils.

LACE

Some famous brides—including Queen Victoria, the mother of the modern white wedding, and actress Grace Kelly—have worn lace gowns, which are becoming popular again. For lace dresses, my favorite flower is the rose. I like thickly petaled garden roses for a bride in head-to-toe Alençon lace, both gown and veil. Lace and roses together are the epitome of romantic style. Named in part for their similarity to this luxurious material, lacecap hydrangea, blue lace scabiosa, and Queen Anne's lace work well as filler details next to the rose as the focal flower.

To match lace, I also like to put together bouquets of small, detailed flowers that resemble the floral patterns on a teacup. The romance and charm of these teacup-inspired bouquets are perfect for a wedding at high noon, when the bright light allows wedding guests to appreciate their delicacy.

Spring is one of the best times for lacy flowers, including lily-of-the-valley, snowball viburnum, andromeda (pieris; late winter–spring), lilac, and astrantia. Lady's mantle is a lacy choice for summer. All year long, bupleurum, baby's breath, and love-in-a-mist (nigella) are perfect lacy fillers.

Left: **GWEN.** *A cotton lace doily frames each rose, and the same lace surrounds the bouquet.* 9-inch wired bouquet of 'Emanuelle' roses and 'Sahara' roses, with cotton lace trim. ♦♦

Right: **ANYA.** *Lily-of-the-valley adds a touch of lacy texture to lovely garden roses.* 12-inch hand-tied bouquet of 'Sahara' and 'Cortes Quatro' roses and lily-of-the-valley (in spring, widely available and half the out-of-season price), trimmed with a simple satin ribbon. In spring ♦♦♦♦ otherwise ♦♦♦♦♦♦

Opposite: **FIORELLA.** *A touch of Alençon lace on the veil complements a bouquet with an ultra-frilly texture.* 12-inch hand-tied bouquet of lilacs (spring), hyacinths (late winter–spring), 'Revue' roses, and sweet peas (spring–early summer). Veil: Kristen Elizabeth; gown: Vera Wang. ♦♦♦

BETHANY. *Soft texture is a classic choice with lace fabrics.* 12-inch hand-tied bouquet of 'Sunny Romantica' roses, 'Jade' roses, 'Carla Romantica' roses, berzelia, and Queen Anne's lace, trimmed with taffeta ribbon. Gown: Kathryn and Alexandra. ♦♦♦

A design inspired BY LOVE-IN-A-MIST, WHICH MIRRORS THE FRINGE ON THE LACE.

RACHEL. 10-inch hand-tied bouquet of 'Sunny Romantica' roses, 'Talea' roses, love-in-a-mist (nigella), muscari, and narcissus (last two best in late winter–spring), trimmed with ⅜-inch velvet ribbon. Gown: Ines di Santo; earrings: private collection. ♦

RUCHING AND PLEATING

Pleated and ruched (gathered) gowns are very flattering and create a curvy silhouette for a thinner bride. A full skirt tufted to create cascading, billowing volume and a ruched bodice decorated with sequins and beading are well complemented by a round bouquet filled with thickly petaled flowers and frilly shapes. The weighty look of Bombay celosia, ruffled carnations, or cabbage roses sets off the shapely form of a bride wearing a gown with glorious tucks and pleats.

For winter, I like to use carnations, kale, and double paperwhites or daffodils to match ruching, and for spring, double tulips, camellia, and fluffy peach blossoms. For summer, I recommend double hollyhocks and garden roses. For fall, I use ranunculus with imported peonies or hydrangeas. The hydrangea, considered "boastful" because of its generous flower power, goes well with the exaggerated style of a ruched gown.

Opposite, left: **FELICIA.** *Tiny roses sewn to the tucks on the ribbon create a cascade of blooms that echo a ruched gown.* 10-inch hand-tied bouquet of hydrangeas, 'Bluebird' roses, and 'Blue Curiosa' roses, with beaded flower accents; it is trimmed with hand-ruched taffeta ribbon with applied faux flowers. You can also wire fresh roses, tack them onto the ribbon the day before the wedding, and store the bouquet in a cooler. ♦♦♦

Opposite, right: **PAULINA.** *Ruching taffeta ribbon is easy.* 9-inch wired bouquet of 'Scentsation' camellia and double daffodils (both spring), trimmed with ruched wired taffeta. I started with 5-inch-wide ribbon, so I had plenty of material to pull into the tucks. ♦♦

This page: **BLYTHE.** *Fruit-colored flowers bring out the gown's oyster-gray tone. Vibrant colors juxtaposed with the ribbon's thick texture create an unexpected look.* 12-inch hand-tied bouquet of Bombay celosia, 'Kirsch Royale' roses, 'Super Green' roses, 'Evelyn' roses, peach carnations, and 'Yves Piaget' roses, trimmed with double-faced satin ribbon. Gown: Ines di Santo. ♦♦♦

Damask

You may be most familiar with damask from the beautiful, rich patterns on tapestry, linens, or wallpaper, but this lush fabric type has become popular with brides. Designers are constructing wedding dresses from golden silk-screened fabrics, lavish embroidered materials, rich woven brocades, and quilted textured material.

For gowns of extensively detailed fabrics, the overall feeling of the bouquet should be very warm. I like to use flowers with lush, heavy color and velvety texture to complement these luxurious materials. Highly scented flowers add another layer of opulence. I also like emblematic flowers and materials, including the ornamental pineapple, cabbage rose, and artichoke—all classic damask motifs. The pineapple symbolizes hospitality, the rose love, and the artichoke hope.

PENELOPE. *Coordinated accessories, as in this matching purse and bouquet, create a smart look.* 10-inch hand-tied bouquet of 'Ranuncula' roses, gerbera daisies, and oscularia succulents. Brocade purse: Inge Christopher. ♦♦♦

Miniature pineapples WITH STRIPED TOPS ARE THE FOCAL POINT OF THIS BOUQUET.

DIANA. 12-inch hand-tied bouquet of 'Shanty' roses, ornamental pineapple, pincushion scabiosa (summer), carnations, and hydrangeas. Gown: Ines di Santo. ♦♦♦

Above: **CECELIA.** *Black and gold tease out the lowlights of 'Black Baccara' roses.* 8- and 9-inch hand-tied bouquets of 'Black Baccara' roses and black kale, trimmed with satin and dupioni silk ribbon. The larger bouquet is accented with 26-gauge gold bullion wire wrapped around a bamboo skewer, the smaller one with a gold and crystal bow-tie ornament. ♦♦

Opposite: **SOFIA.** 14-inch hand-tied bouquet of 'Annabelle' hydrangeas (summer–fall), ranunculus (year-round, but best in spring and fall), Auricula primrose (spring), 'Hocus Pocus' roses, black artichoke, and acacia (mimosa; winter–spring), trimmed with hand-ruffled dotted organdy ribbon. ♦♦♦♦

Group similar flowers TOGETHER IN A MIXED BOUQUET FOR A LUSH LOOK.

PRETTY BOWS

Bows are a fun starting point in a bouquet design. A large bow on the crown of your veil, tiny bows down the back of your dress, or big bows on your shoes might be inspirations. You can place bows in the bouquet to complement the bows on your gown, or if your dress has a single large bow on the bodice, it might be best just to put a big bow on the handle. To match bows, I like prim and feminine flowers—roses, hydrangeas, orchids, stephanotis. Graceful bows of a vibrant color can add style to an all-white bouquet.

Above, left: **AUDREY**. *To add a surprising element to this prim, clean bouquet, I folded blades of lily grass into bows and held them in place with 3-inch glass-headed pins.* 10-inch hand-tied bouquet of 'Citronella' roses, euphorbia, stephanotis, and lily grass. Shoes: Joey O; monogram: Filigree Monograms. ♦♦♦

Above, right: **JULIET**. *Tiny bows on the trailing ribbon echo bows on the back of the bride's gown.* 11-inch hand-tied bouquet of 'Sweet Moments' roses, "antiqued" hydrangeas (fall), and smoke bush trimmed with 5-inch taffeta ribbon with 2-inch double-faced satin overlay, punctuated with 5/8-inch grosgrain ribbon bows. Tie 6-inch pieces of the grosgrain ribbon into evenly spaced bows around the length of the satin ribbon, securing them with a stitch on the back side. Layer the satin ribbon on top of the taffeta ribbon, holding it in place with intermittent securing stitches. ♦♦♦

Opposite: **CALISTA**. *Tuberoses are not showy but smell wonderful. Their neutral color makes them a pretty filler for peach roses.* 12-inch hand-tied bouquet of 'Talea' roses, pee gee hydrangeas that have turned green (late fall), and tuberoses, trimmed with 3-inch embroidered ribbon. In spring, substitute other green hydrangeas for pee gees; in summer, use guilder rose viburnum. ♦♦♦♦

Sweet Perfume

Whether sweet or spicy, scent can be one of a flower's most captivating qualities. A bride may not remember every detail of her bouquet, but she is unlikely to forget its scent. Smell is said to be the sense with the strongest link to memory, and memories related to scent may be more emotional than those linked with vision or hearing. The woman who chooses her bouquet with her nose is a true romantic at heart.

Test your affinity for certain scents before committing to one or more for your bouquet. With your florist, take a tour of a flower market for a firsthand whiff of different flowers. Or ask her to suggest a flower scent similar to your favorite perfume.

Not all cut flowers have a detectable scent. Many hybrids, such as the modern tea rose, are virtually odorless (scent can be lost as flowers are bred for color, stem length, vase life, and form). But there are plenty of scented blooms available. My favorite, the tuberose, has a complex scent that is highly prized as a base for perfume; while not spectacular in form, it's available year-round, and a couple of stems will fill your bouquet with lovely scent. Stephanotis, which in the early twentieth century replaced the easily bruised orange blossom as the most popular flower for a bridal crown, has a rich scent, and I use it often. Old-fashioned garden roses produce a diffuse, yet rich and intoxicating aroma. Cattleya orchids smell exotic, honey-sweet, and sublime. The gardenia may be the most romantic scented flower. Stock, widely available in a range of colors and one of the least expensive scented flowers, has a sugary sweet scent.

I carried sweet peas in my bouquet, and I will always have a deep affection for their delicate, sweet smell. Peonies are fruity-sweet and make my nose happy. Muscari and sweet violets smell like candy. The crisp scent of hyacinth is a harbinger of spring. Lily-of-the-valley is expensive out of season, but worth it for its scent; when its cost is lower in mid-spring, I buy it for brides who love its distinct, grassy-floral scent.

BRIDAL AROMATHERAPY

Besides creating memories, your scented bouquet can serve as a personal aromatherapy device. A nervous bride might carry sprigs of lavender, geranium, or jasmine in order to feel more relaxed as she walks down the aisle. Someone shy could choose sprigs of rosemary or juniper to perk her up before the reception. The exhausted bride could benefit from the pick-me-up of fresh spearmint, and one who fears experiencing a bout of pre-wedding blues might lift her spirits with scented roses or marigolds.

VIOLA. *Sweet, anise-scented violets don't last long in a vase, but they work well for a one-day event like a wedding.* **10-inch hand-tied bouquet of violets (early spring) and 'Sensation' lilacs (early spring).** *Violets are very delicate; keep them in water until just before the ceremony. They can be hard to find as a cut flower. I got these from Año Nuevo, a small family farm in California.* Gown: Elizabeth Fillmore; diamond necklace: Saks Fifth Avenue. ♦♦

Flower Fragrances

Heady, sweet, and pungent

Very strong
Armandii clematis · Genista
Korean viburnum
Madonna lily · Oriental lily
Plumeria
Strong
'Naked Lady' Amaryllis
Eucharis lily

Fruity sweet—delicate grape or citrus

Very strong
Hyacinth · Winter daphne
Strong
Lilac · Peony · Violet
Moderate
Lemon balm · Muscari · 'Sweet Perfumela' rose · Sweet pea

Richly sweet—delicious honey, vanilla, etc.

Very strong
Honeysuckle · Narcissus
Strong
Cattleya orchid · Heliotrope (cherry vanilla) · Lavender · Stock Zygopetalum orchid (vanilla)
Moderate
Chocolate-scented geranium
Magnolia · Rosemary · 'Sherry Baby' oncidium orchid (chocolate)
Light
Cymbidium orchid · Vanda and mokara orchids (vanilla)

Robust floral—intoxicating, seductive

Very strong
Gardenia · 'Gertrude Jekyl' rose
Jasmine · Stephanotis
'Sterling Silver' rose
Tuberose · 'Yves Piaget' rose

Spicy sweet—pepper, clove

Very strong
Boronia
Strong
Freesia
Moderate
Marigold · Pittosporum
Light
Carnation · Hypericum (coffee)
Pepperberry
Very light
Kale

Grassy sweet or pollen

Very strong
Forsythia · Lily-of-the-valley
Moderate
Acacia (mimosa) · Calendula
Feverfew · Yarrow
Light
Asclepias (butterfly weed)
Chrysanthemum · Marguerite daisy
Very light
Sunflower

Balsam sweet—mellow, woody

Moderate
Artemisia · Bay leaf · Eucalyptus
Evergreen · Sage
Santolina · Scented geranium
Thyme

Fresh and sweet—stimulating

Moderate
Spearmint
Light
Bells of Ireland
Very light
Dahlia · Hydrangea · Snapdragon
Tulip

52 ❦ BOUQUET CHIC

Stephanotis wreath

Lily-of-the-valley

Gardenia

Freesia

Cattleya orchid

Stock

'Sweet Perfumela' rose

Stephanotis

Peony

Fragrant White Flowers. Nature bestows the most intoxicating of scents on the most delicate white flowers.

IF YOU'RE ALLERGIC . . .

Even though many flowers are scentless, if you are extremely sensitive you may want to use silk flowers. Today, beautiful specimens are available that are botanically correct and lifelike. Many of the bouquets in this book can be replicated with silks. Glue a few crystals on the petals of silk flowers to give them a "dew-kissed" glow.

A Bit of Sparkle

Inserts—jewels on long prongs inserted directly among the flowers—are an easy way to make a bouquet shine. You can also wire a real brooch, beaded flowers, or earrings onto long stems and insert them into a bouquet. Some brides may like to keep their look understated and use "sparkle" only on the bouquet's stem—with, say, a small glittery pin.

JEWELED GLAMOUR

Diamonds, crystals, sequins, and glitter are no longer just for beauty pageants and cocktail parties. Faceted crystal beads, shimmering rhinestones, and sequins are now applied liberally to wedding gowns. And a bride wearing giant crystal chandelier earrings, a glittering choker necklace, or a "bling-bling" brooch on a plain gown needs a bouquet that is as brilliant as her other accessories. The idea is to design a bouquet to match the jeweled glamour—not compete with it. If the sparkle is all whites, understated color with intense glitter works beautifully. I recommend a small bouquet with pale color and lots of dazzle, and then use bouquet jewels, jewelry, or glitter on the flowers to jazz it up. For the bride who will wear bold, colorful jewelry accents, I again make the floral ensemble small but as fancy as the jewelry she is wearing. When the bouquet essentially becomes another piece of jewelry, an 8-inch posy can pack a lot of pizzazz. Waxy flowers—orchids, hyacinths, polished tea roses (like 'Sweet Akito'), stephanotis—work well with the crispness of shiny jewels.

Left: **KENDRA.** *Tiny Swarovski crystals inserted into the centers of stephanotis create a magical effect. 7-inch wired stephanotis bouquet, trimmed with hand-ruched organdy ribbon.* ♦♦♦

Right: **EYDIE.** *The colors of the flowers bring out the blue sparkle in the ribbon and brooch. 8-inch hand-tied bouquet of hydrangeas, sweet peas (spring–early summer), stephanotis, and zinnias (summer), trimmed with embellished organdy layered with ruffled organdy ribbon. Brooch: vintage; necklace in foreground: Michal Negrin.* ♦♦♦

HELENA. *Buy glittered roses or lightly glitter them yourself.* 8-inch hand-tied bouquet of glittered 'Akito' roses and hydrangeas, trimmed with dupioni silk ribbon. Tiny crystal buckles are attached to the stem on silk ribbons. To add glitter to roses, spritz them with spray adhesive, immediately sprinkle on iridescent "pixie dust" sparkles, let dry for a minute or so, and shake off the excess. Gown: Anne Barge. ♦♦

JESSICA. *Gems inserted on prongs add sparkle, as does a crystal hair brooch pushed up into the wires of the bouquet.* 8-inch wired bouquet of Hawaiian dendrobium orchids and 'Jade' roses, with a ribbon of double-faced satin. Dendrobium orchids have a distinctive look that depends on where they are grown (Thailand and Hawaii are the two main sources). I used Hawaiian dendrobiums because of their shape. Gown: Badgley Mischka; brooch: Voletta Couture. ♦♦♦♦

A bouquet accented WITH SWAROVSKI CRYSTALS LOOKS LIKE IT WAS JUST PULLED OUT OF THE JEWELRY CASE.

ELEGANT PEARLS

If the bride will wear pearls—a strand around the neck, accents on a veil, trim on her gown's bodice—I make those perfect little treasures the starting point for the bouquet. Pearls project a refined elegance, and stephanotis has a waxy texture and natural white color that wonderfully matches theirs. When you wire stephanotis (see Chapter 1), you can place a pearl accent in the center of each blossom. Stephanotis blossoms can also be strung— like pearls!—in a long, trailing accent. For a late fall bride, the pearl-like snowberry may be the perfect bouquet accent. Fleshy, round snowberries come in ivory white or blushing pink. I mix them with roses for a garden-fresh, yet sophisticated look. Mount large ones on long metal stems available at specialty florists and insert them between blossoms, or incorporate pearl-headed pins in your bouquet's ribbon stem wrap.

Above: **GRACE.** *Deep olive green and blush flowers are classy with white or pinkish pearls.* 9-inch hand-tied bouquet of 'Vendela' and 'Akito' roses, blush snowberries (late fall), moss on a stick (a.k.a. Indian Pon Pon), and white mini cymbidium orchids, trimmed with 2-inch balsam-green, double-faced satin ribbon; Veil: Madina Vadache. ♦♦♦

Right: **CAROLINE.** *Sophisticated pearls make a neutral-toned bouquet spectacular. The swirling pattern of a nautilus shell inspired this design.* 12-inch hand-tied bouquet of 'Bianca Candy' roses and 'Geneve' roses, trimmed with 3-inch viscose ribbon. Gown and veil: Madina Vadache. ♦♦♦♦

The bolero INSPIRED THE DESIGN OF THIS CLASSIC BOUQUET.

KATHERINE. 10-inch wired bouquet of stephanotis and 'Akito' roses, with a strung stephanotis cascade and 1-inch taupe picot edge satin ribbon. Gown and bolero: Saison Blanche. ◆◆◆◆◆◆

A Primer on Roses

Of the many flowers and floral styles that remain immune to fashion trends, the most notable is the rose—a constant worldwide favorite and the classic choice of brides. Here's a quick rundown of the types of roses available as cut flowers:

HYBRID TEA. The most familiar shape—a classic long-stemmed, high-centered rose. The modern hybrid tea rose exists in many varieties, with differences in color, petal count and shape, and stem length. For example, 'Vendela' is an elegant ivory champagne rose with a high center, and 'Talea' is peachy-cream and sports ruffled petals.

GARDEN ROSES. Damask, gallica, and peony-style. Many of these "old-fashioned" roses are delicate and short-stemmed. Often strongly scented, they feature many petals.

SPRAY OR FLORIBUNDA. Small roses with multiple heads per stem.

SWEETHEART. Roses with very small heads and short stems.

Rose growers respond to changes in fashion and regularly introduce new varieties in combinations of color, shape, size, scent, and other characteristics. Because developing a rose variety is a significant economic undertaking, as new roses are being introduced growers do not retire existing varieties (though they may reduce production), so the total number and diversity of rose varieties is constantly increasing. While only a small percentage of all developed varieties are in full production as cut flowers at any given time, there is great diversity in today's market. Consumers have tremendous choice and, with diligent research, should be able to find what they want or something very close to it. U.S. consumers can choose from roses grown in this country (most are produced in California) or imported from Canada, South America, Mexico, and Holland. Europeans use the same source locales plus Africa and Israel. In the U.S., the VeriFlora® label certifies cut flowers, from here and abroad, that meet standards of quality and social and environmental responsibility.

MAKING A DUCHESS ROSE BOUQUET

A duchess rose is a very large "composite" rose formed from the petals of many roses. Start with a single large rose on a stem and detached petals from other rose heads. Then follow the steps given below.

DUCHESS ROSE BOUQUET. Shown are duchess roses of 'Esperance' and 'Big Fun' roses.

Step 1. Create clusters of petals by wiring 3 or 4 rose petals laid one on top of the other. Bend the wire first and then insert it into the face of the petals.

Step 2. Place several layers of wired petal clusters (4 or 5 clusters per layer) around the central rose. Tape each layer individually, binding the wires to the main rose stem.

Step 3. Make the rose as large as you want. Make one large, glorious rose, or tape multiple roses together to make a Duchess rose bouquet.

METALLIC SHIMMER

They say never to "gild the lily," but I like bending the rules a little. Embellishing even an orchid can be tastefully done. Wearing one metallic accessory—shiny, pearlized shoes, a lamé clutch purse, a thick gold necklace, orchids lightly dusted with pixie glitter—is going just to the top without going over. Muted shades of silver, gold, bronze, and copper are beautiful accents for just about any color. Make a simple and elegant statement by wrapping ivory roses and astilbe with a metallic silver or deep antique gold ribbon.

It can be nice to use metallic colors in the bouquet to complement metallic colors on the gown or in the jewelry. Berzelia berries and foliage like artemisia, dusty miller, eucalyptus, silver tree, and lamb's ear can contribute icy silver tones. Match rich gold tones with harvest yellow or brown roses or cymbidium orchids. If your dress is platinum, you don't have to carry silver flowers—warm and cool shades of colors can complement platinum beautifully. For a cool, sterling silver dress I suggest icy light pinks, butter yellow, crisp blues, gray-lavenders, dark plums, or cappuccino browns.

For a warm, golden champagne dress, stick with colors like warm mauve, burgundy, peach, flame red, and chocolate brown. All-white with a hint of metallic is always stylish and elegant; a small touch of silver foliage stunningly accents an all-white bouquet. I also love mixing metallic colors for an eclectic look, like golden orchids with silvery foliages.

DESTINY. *For a glitzy golden look, spritz spray adhesive on petal edges and sprinkle glitter over them.* 12-inch-long cascade bouquet of premium cymbidium orchids with applied glitter, trimmed with double-faced satin ribbon with gold lamé lace overlay. Each flower in the cascade is hand-wired with #20 gauge wire to hold the shape. Gown and scarf: Pronovias. ♦♦♦♦

Dress up long hair THAT IS WORN "DOWN" WITH A BEAUTIFUL FLORAL CROWN.

STEPHANIE. 18-inch arm bouquet of calla lilies, mini calla lilies, and silver tree. This face-framing crown of wired stephanotis and pearls has trailing sides that enhance the bride's beautiful long hair. Gown: Vera Wang. ♦♦♦♦♦ (with crown)

This book is all about bouquets that represent a bride's dream—the quintessential fantasy of "happily ever after." To create a bouquet that captures this blissful spirit, I combine diffuse textures with lacy shapes that project a dream-like quality—perfect for the bride who wants to feel as though she is walking on a cloud.

Left: SADIE. *Beautiful neutral shades complement a gown's gorgeous ivory ruffles.* 14-inch crescent-shaped, hand-wired bouquet of hyacinths (late winter–spring), 'Broadway' and 'Xotica' oriental lilies, santolinas, carnations, nerine lilies, 'Camel' roses, 'Emanuelle' roses, and andromeda (pieris; late winter–spring). This bouquet of peach and celadon emits a sweet, dreamy scent that is a mix of herbal (from the santolina), fruit (hyacinth), floral (lily), and spicy (carnation). Gown: Enmanuel Couture. ♦♦♦

Right: SADIE TIARA. *A coronet of delicate blossoms makes the bride into a fairy-tale princess.* The tiara is made up of hyacinths (late winter–spring), santolinas, and andromeda (pieris; late winter–spring).

The heavy texture OF ASTILBE GIVES THIS BOUQUET A DREAMY QUALITY.

ANNA. 16-inch hand-tied bouquet of blush
Hawaiian dendrobium orchids, stock, astilbe,
'Rosita Vendela' roses, and 'Talea' roses.
Gown: Kathryn and Alexandra. ♦ ♦ ♦ ♦

FRANCINE. *A eucalyptus armature supports a delicious spray of delicate orchids.* 14-inch hand-tied bouquet of phalaenopsis orchids and seeded eucalyptus. This is a nice, light bouquet for its size. Gown: Sally Crew. ♦♦♦♦

3

Something New: Contemporary Looks

WHEN A BRIDE SAYS SHE WANTS SOMETHING "NEW" AND "DIFFERENT," I ASK HER IF she wants something different from her friends' bouquets or a more innovative look. What it usually comes down to is she wants to be original in an elegant way. Innovative bridal bouquets feature discovery (newly developed or unusual flowers), surprise (fresh colors and textures, or unexpected shapes), and exploration (flowers that suit an unusual locale).

Today a bride may stand barefoot on the beach or walk across a grassy lawn or down a cobbled path. For adventuresome brides, the fashion industry has created dresses with lighter-weight fabrics, sexier cuts, and avant-garde details. For weddings among a cathedral of pines, in a snowy mountain lodge, or atop an oceanside bluff, it is wise to let Mother Nature help determine the floral style. A bouquet carried through the woods should be harmonious with the quiet, dark natural surroundings, while cool crisp colors are best for a seaside wedding.

If you have a new idea in mind, consult with a professional early. And if you want a florist to create an out-of-the-ordinary style, look for someone with a flair for the dramatic.

FLOWERS FOR THE DARING BRIDE

Today's horticulturalists produce flowers in soft pastels, riots of bright color, exotic dark hues, and interesting variegations. They offer funky new textures and shapes, including oddball flowers like toad lilies, furry allium 'Hair' seed heads, pods and grasses, even orchids that look like spiders. Hydrangeas and peonies, traditionally found only in summer, are now available in winter from the Southern Hemisphere. "Spring" bulbs are grown year-round in hothouses in my home state of Washington and in Holland and Canada. Exotic brunia and kangaroo paw are readily available from South Africa and New Zealand. New rose colors are constantly introduced, like fashions on the runway.

Keeping It Beautiful

Brides looking for something "new and different" need to take care. An innovative design philosophy can startle or reject tradition entirely, but a bride must be wary of wild ideas or the "flower du jour," and instead choose flowers (their color, line, and texture, and the shape of the bouquet) that suit the wedding's location and that enhance the scale, cut, and texture of her dress. The best bouquets accentuate dress details in a natural way, even when the bride is wearing a gown of tiered, striped, shirred or knotted fabrics. If the dress is sleek and modern, I am inclined to accentuate the simple lines. If it has a couture element, such as ostrich feather appliqué, or is cut above the knee (a "mini" dress), the bouquet design should match or complement it. My motto is "Have fun, but keep it beautiful."

ELEGANT LINES

Many modern gown styles use geometric shapes, asymmetries, and stark contrasts. For bouquets to accompany them, I prefer patterns and lines that the eye can follow and that create depth and rhythm. I love including streaks of color with striped grasses or creating three-dimensional effects with wood ting-ting. In some of my designs, colors and shapes run through the bouquet like a ribbon. And I create a lot of bouquets with knotted foliage or sleeves of woven grasses.

ABIGAIL. *Wood ting-ting echoes the lines in the bride's veil.* 8-inch hand-tied bouquet of parrot tulips (spring) and wood ting-ting. Buy wood ting-ting at a florist or a craft store. Gown: Luly Yang Couture; veil: Madina Vadache. ♦

CASSIDY. *This bouquet would look great with a bride wearing a spiky updo.* 11-inch hand-tied bouquet of New Zealand flax leaves, mini calla lilies, berzelia, 'Riverdale' roses, and 'Pacific Blue' roses, trimmed with 1 1/2-inch striped taffeta ribbon. ♦ ♦ ♦

MAKING AN "EDGY" CASSIDY BOUQUET

The Cassidy bouquet is a great design for a bride wearing her hair in a spiky up-do.

Step 1. Split each flax leaf down the spine by pulling it apart. Remove the spine.

Step 2. Tie a knot halfway down the length of the leaf. Bring the free end around and through the knot. Pull tightly and insert a dab of floral glue into the center of the knot.

Step 3. Make the rose as large as you want. Make one large, glorious rose, or tape multiple roses together to make a Duchess rose bouquet.

Step 4. Clip the ends of the flax at a 45-degree angle with sharp shears. Allow about 2 inches of the leaf to stick out

Soft Textures

The plant world is full of soft textures, especially in fall, when grasses produce a wide array of inflorescences (flower spikes) that look like feathers. If you want softness in the spring and summer, you can always incorporate feathers into a bridal bouquet to soften its lines. Also in the spring, a soft-textured gown looks great with soft, spidery gerbera daisies or fringed tulips that are frayed and look like they have been given a razor cut. "Chopped-up" petals diffuse light in an elegant way.

Above, left: **SEPHORA.** *Fringed tulips diffuse the light in a soft and elegant way.* 10-inch hand-tied bouquet of fringed tulips, nerine lilies, and dyed ostrich feathers. ♦♦

Above, right: **GENEVIEVE.** *Stems of pampas grass inflorescence taped upside down around a bouquet's base make a stunning "feathery" wrap.* 8-inch wired bouquet of cymbidium orchids, rattlesnake grass, and pampas grass (last two, late summer–fall), trimmed with picot double-faced satin ribbon. ♦♦

Opposite: **AVA.** 10-inch hand-tied bouquet of assorted spidery gerbera daisies, trimmed with eyelash wire ribbon. Self-adhesive Austrian crystals are available at specialty florist supply stores, but you can also buy crystals at a craft store and glue them on. Gown: Madina Vadache. ♦♦

Small Austrian crystals IN THE FLOWER CENTERS MATCH TINY DETAILS ON THE GOWN.

Appealing Patterns

Gowns with stripes, dots, and checks are great fun to match with flowers. Bright, happy jewel tones or spirited sorbet pastels look beautiful with patterned gowns. I like to use globular flowers—hypericum, craspedia, coneflower pods—with dots. Roses or tulips with variegation or tipped in color nicely complement stripes and checks. You can find pattern in the centers of cymbidium orchids, the swirl of fern curls, and the striped and speckled centers of oriental lilies.

A bouquet's ribbon trim can link the bouquet with the dress pattern. Happy taffetas, jacquards, and grosgrains are my favorite ribbon choices with preppie patterns.

Left: **TOVA.** *This fun bouquet looks great when the bride wears a simple dress with a small stripe or geometric detail.* 12-inch hand-tied bouquet of 'Marmalade' roses, 'Sweet Akito' roses, pyracantha berries, frosted mini pinecones, and 'Gertrude Jekyl' roses, trimmed with a 3¼-inch striped taffeta ribbon to which ⅛-inch gingham ribbon bows are attached. ♦♦♦

Center: **SIMONE.** *The polka-dot pattern of the ribbon wrap echoes the black centers of the anemones.* 10-inch hand-tied bouquet of Dutch anemones (fall–spring), wrapped with ⅞-inch polka-dot grosgrain ribbon. I left the stems exposed for a "just-picked" garden look. ♦♦

Right: **TYREE.** *If the groom will wear a kilt—or even just a colorful striped tie—you might want to design your bouquet to match.* 10-inch hand-tied bouquet of 'Shanty' roses, bi-color hydrangeas, flame celosia (late summer–fall), sea hollies (eryngium), and carnations, trimmed with a 1½-inch tartan taffeta ribbon. ♦♦

JILL. *To enhance this sweet bouquet, wear a chunky round, beaded necklace in a bright orange or berry tone.* 12-inch hand-tied bouquet of 'Cherries Jubilee' red spray roses, 'Cherry Brandy' orange bi-color roses, peach striped roses, cymbidium orchids, hypericum, echinacea (coneflower) pods, and smoke bush, trimmed with 1½-inch dotted jacquard ribbon. Gown: Madina Vadache. ♦♦♦♦

Truly, Madly, Deeply

In Victorian days, brides swallowed a marigold dipped in rose water as an aphrodisiac before the wedding. If you have chosen a low-cut neckline or a high hem for your dress, you may have no problem feeling enticing. Yet most brides want to feel not just sexy but all-around beautiful for the ceremony. The sweetness of flowers can bring balance to an alluring style.

Feminine Charms

Wearing a full ball gown with a low cut in front or a full cutaway in back, with many lacy frills and sequins? Add charm to the look with powderpuff dahlias or sweet peas; both are child-like and coy. Other flowers for a corset gown or one inspired by lingerie might include romantic daisy feverfew or sweet violets. Angelic blue hydrangeas are another pretty choice for the "girly-girl" bride.

Left: **LYNETTE.** *To add flair to luxurious, scented white flowers, give them a little blushing color by spritzing lightly with floral paint.* 10-inch hand-tied bouquet of hydrangeas, stephanotis, and gardenias (the last two lightly dusted with floral paint); the bouquet is trimmed with 2-inch pleated organdy ribbon. Gown, shoes, and necklace: Luly Yang Couture. ♦♦♦

Right: **DULCE.** *Sophisticated, feminine giant peonies ring small, sweet ranunculus (like fruit candies)—perhaps for a bride who is mature but still young at heart.* 12-inch hand-tied bouquet of peonies (fall–spring) and ranunculus (year-round, but best in spring and fall). The stems have been "petal-wrapped" with ruched viscose ribbon; see page 33 for instructions. ♦♦♦♦

A look that's A MIX OF SWEET AND SEXY.

MIRABELLE. 14-inch hand-tied bouquet of dahlias (best summer–fall), 'Evelyn' and Juliette Drouet roses, stephanotis, and lisianthus, trimmed with viscose ribbon. Gown: Saison Blanche. ♦♦♦♦

Bold Contrasts

For brides who are drawn to the cool sophistication of more "masculine" styles—warm colors, sharp lines, bold contrasts—I recommend wood tones, spices, and tropical flowers. Hard accents like metallic bullion wires add an architectural look to the softness of roses. Ribbon patterns that take off from tie and ascot prints add a refined yet commanding look to a bouquet. Many waxy tropical flowers—glossy anthuriums, flaming ostrich plume ginger, bright and rigid birds of paradise, bold orchids—are associated with aggressiveness and bravado. Matching one such waxy flower with a softer flower makes for an interesting combination, such as anthuriums with amaranthus.

Left: **BRANDY.** *Bonfire roses are fashionable and modern. Deep brick-red and caramel are spicy, stunning, and bold, a perfect base for a rich copper-wire accent.* 10-inch hand-tied bouquet of 'Bonfire' roses, trimmed with shantung dupioni silk ribbon. The exterior of the bouquet is wrapped with #26 gauge copper wire, available at most craft stores. Wrap the wire around the bouquet as you would wrap yarn around a ball shape, stretching it out slightly. Join the ends of the wire and tape them onto the bouquet's handle, and wrap the handle with ribbon. ♦♦

Right: **TAYLOR.** *Ribbon inspired by an ascot gives this bouquet a masculine touch.* 10-inch hand-tied bouquet of 'Terra Cotta' roses, 'Coup Soleil' roses, and cattleya orchids, trimmed with shantung dupioni silk ribbon with an ascot print. ♦♦♦

Hard lines & SOFT TEXTURES COMBINE TO MATCH THE BRIDE'S JACKET,
INSPIRED BY ENGLISH RIDING GEAR.

VALERIE. 12-inch hand-tied
bouquet with long-stemmed
anthuriums, amaranthus (summer–
fall), epidendrum orchids, celosia
(late summer–fall), and wood
ting-ting, trimmed with striped
dupioni silk ribbon. If you can't find
epidendrum orchids, substitute
bouvardia. Gown: Madina Vadache;
jacket: Cicada Bridal. ♦♦♦

Wedding Destinations

Not all brides are married in a church or even their hometown. If you will wed in a non-traditional locale—the coast, the tropics, the desert, a woodland, a garden—let your surroundings inspire your look, including your flowers.

The Seaside Ceremony

Every coastal locale has its distinct colors. Whether you will repeat your vows on the deck of a yacht off St. Tropez, on the sands of Maui, or dockside on the cool waters of the Great Lakes, the tones of your wedding can range from beaming azures to subdued gray-blues. Small details—pearls, pieces of coral, a rose constructed of Capiz shells—are great for water-themed bouquets, and I love to use cool, calm blue-greens at waterside events.

Left: **KELSEY.** *A design suggested by the colors of the Pacific Northwest coast.* 10-inch hand-tied bouquet of 'Mari Romantica' roses, sea holly (eryngium), and "antiqued" hydrangeas (fall), trimmed with 1½-inch striped grosgrain and 1-inch silk ribbon. If your wedding is not in the fall, spritz blue hydrangeas with green flower paint. ♦♦♦

Right: **NERINA.** *In a bouquet inspired by white sand beaches, nerine lilies echo coral, and winterbud looks like sea fan.* Hairpiece and 12-inch hand-tied bouquet of green ranunculus (year-round, but best in spring and fall), lace coral, assorted shells, 'Sahara' roses, nerine lilies, and winterbud, trimmed with organdy ribbon. Gown: Elizabeth Fillmore. ♦♦♦

Left, top: **HALEY.** *A beachy madras pattern suggested this look.* 14-inch hand-tied bouquet of 'First Lady' roses, 'Geisha' roses, hydrangeas, stock, euphorbia (spring), and gladiolus blossoms. ♦♦♦

Left, bottom: **LISLE.** *Caribbean colors permeate this bouquet.* 12-inch arm-held, hand-tied bouquet of phalaenopsis orchids, 'Bwwig Fun' roses, 'Esperance' roses, 'Rosita Vendela' roses, anthuriums, and assorted seashells, trimmed with 2-inch double-faced satin ribbon. ♦♦♦♦

Right: **MORGAN.** *In this bouquet, inspired by the colors of a sleepy northern harbor, pincushion proteas match the skirt's spray design.* 12-inch hand-tied pincushion proteas, 'Leah Romantica' roses, 'Vendela' roses, ranunculus (year-round, but best in spring and fall), and roses made from Capiz shells, trimmed with silk-satin ribbon. Gown: Cicada Bridal. ♦♦♦

THE LUSH LOOK OF THE TROPICS

If you will invite your wedding guests to a tropical locale, you can base your bouquet on local flowers that may be quite different from those available at home. Consult with a florist at your destination to learn what's possible. The blazing sun and warm breezes of the tropics are the perfect context for a very bright, even "surreal" color scheme. In those latitudes, a bouquet of fuchsia orchids trimmed with turquoise blue ribbon does not look brash—it's "of a piece" with the surroundings. If you don't want bright colors, more understated pink, white, or green orchids also work well.

Or perhaps you want to bring a little "destination wedding" flavor to your hometown. There are no rules that say you cannot have the colors and flowers of Tahiti for your ceremony in Missoula.

Far left, top: **ILIANA.** *Electric cattleya orchids, imported from Thailand, brighten this bouquet.* 10-inch wired bouquet of 'Milva' roses, cattleya orchids, and delphinium blossoms, trimmed with double-faced satin and capriccio ribbon. ♦♦♦

Far left, bottom: **ULANI.** *This bouquet has an exotic look. Bombay celosia beautifully echoes a coral reef.* 10-inch hand-tied bouquet of Bombay celosia, 'Karadise' roses, and 'Amsterdam' roses, trimmed with 2-inch moiré taffeta ribbon. ♦♦♦

Near left: **MALIA.** *For a bouquet of tropical fruit colors, a ribbon suggests azure skies and gently breaking, clear blue surf.* 10-inch wired bouquet of cattleya orchids and gerbera daisies, trimmed with grosgrain ribbon sewn in a ruched or crinkled fashion. Gown: Sally Crew. ♦♦♦

Above: **APHRODITE.** *I was thinking of pink Hawaiian sunsets as I designed this bouquet.* 12-inch hand-tied, arm-held bouquet of pink ostrich plume ginger, tulip anthuriums, 'Rosita Vendela' roses, and mini calla lilies. Ginger, a common tropical flower imported from Hawaii, is readily available on the mainland. ♦♦♦♦

THE DESERT'S STARK BEAUTY

The bride who marries among cacti or canyons in a sleek, bias-cut sheath might choose a bouquet that reflects the landscape's natural rusts and turquoise. One who ties the knot at a hot desert resort could wear a dress beaded in sandy golden tones and carry a bouquet of fiery blooms accented with a beautiful palm-tree jewel.

Left: **SEDONA**. *The colors of the Southwest shine through in this stunning bouquet.* 10-inch hand-tied bouquet of flame calla lilies and 'Sahara' taupe roses, trimmed with 1 1/2-inch ombre taffeta ribbon. ♦♦

Right: **SOLEIL**. *These colors recall the oasis and desert—think Palm Springs and Las Vegas.* 11-inch hand-tied bouquet of 'Juliette' orange roses, white spray roses, scabiosa pods (summer-fall), echeveria, flame calla lilies, and heuchera leaves. ♦♦♦

I created THIS BOUQUET AFTER A VISIT TO THE RED CASTLES OF THE UTAH DESERT.

AMANI. 10-inch hand-tied bouquet of 'Naranja' roses, 'Terranova' roses, oscularia succulents, muscari (late winter–spring), and ivy. Gown: Jenny Packham. ♦♦♦

A Wedding in the Woods

For enchanting and fantastical woodland weddings, I like bouquets that look as if they were lifted from the forest floor. Soft, rich, and earthy in texture, quiet in color, and loose in shape, they might be composed of berries, twigs, vines, seed heads, mosses, or boughs of greenery.

Left: **SYLVIA**. *A thin strand of fluffy yarn winds through this bouquet, inspired by a briar patch. Tiny pieces of lichen on wires add texture.* 11-inch hand-tied bouquet of unripe blackberries, 'Mystery' roses, dendrobium orchids, lichen, and curly willow. The ensemble rests on an armature of pliable willow branches. Mossy-looking yarn wraps the stem. The floral components are available year-round, but most reliably in late summer. Unripe blackberries can be found in the late summer but are available as a specialty item from the cut flower market year-round. ♦♦

Center: **OPHELIA**. *Viburnum berries, with their oak-shaped leaves, make a pretty ensemble with roses.* 12-inch hand-tied bouquet of viburnum berries (summer–fall), 'Cherry Brandy' roses, 'Splendid Renate' roses, and hanging amaranthus (summer–fall), trimmed with 4-inch moiré taffeta ribbon. ♦♦♦

Right: **SAMANTHA**. *A concoction of the herbal and the woodsy.* 11-inch hand-tied bouquet of geraniums, hosta leaves, hellebore (best late fall–early spring), 'Jade' roses, and feathers. The stem is wrapped with mossy green ostrich feather trim, available at fabric stores. ♦♦♦

Mostly greenery & LIGHTWEIGHT
FOR ITS SIZE—A FANTASY-INSPIRED BOUQUET.

FAYE. 14-inch hand-tied bouquet of plumosa fern, black podacarpus, hellebore (best late fall–early spring), orchids, hypericum, and 'Jade' roses. Velvet cape: Kathryn and Alexandra. ♦♦

GETTING MARRIED IN A GARDEN

A paved walkway or formal garden plaza might suggest a more formal look, while if your setting includes a natural garden path covered with rose petals, you may want a casual style. Silk flower appliqués and embroidered designs of colorful vines and blossoms are perfect for a garden wedding dress. Glorious accessories—a crown of flowers, a giant brimmed hat, a ruffled vintage pagoda umbrella—are appropriate romantic touches. Loose lines and lacy tendrils are fitting complements for a garden wedding dress. And don't limit your bouquet to pure "flower power." Flowing greenery enhances the natural style of any garden bouquet.

Left and top right: **EDEN.** *A bride carries a beautiful umbrella whose peachy tones match the floral pinks. The umbrella's ruffles match the trim on the bustled train.* 10-inch hand-tied bouquet of blushing bride, 'Elektra' roses, hypericum, and bupleurum, trimmed with 1½-inch wired double-faced satin ribbon. Gown: Madina Vadache; vintage umbrella: Bella Umbrella. ♦♦

Bottom, right: **MARY.** *For this bouquet I used some of my favorite garden flowers: chocolate cosmos and dusty miller.* 11-inch hand-tied bouquet of ranunculus (year-round, but best in spring and fall), 'Bianca Candy' roses, dusty miller, 'Annabelle' hydrangeas (summer–fall), and chocolate cosmos, trimmed with calico fabric, organdy, and double-faced satin ribbon. Can substitute "Popcorn" ('Ayesha') hydrangeas (summer–fall) or green snowball viburnum for 'Annabelle' hydrangeas. ♦♦♦

Japanese anemones BLEND WITH THE GOWN'S EMBROIDERY.

CARMELA. 14-inch hand-tied bouquet of Japanese anemones (late summer–fall), with giant variegated ivy trailing to the knee. Designed to carry on the arm. Gown: Cicada Bridal. ♦♦♦

Flora and Fauna

If you'll wear fur trim, a fur stole, or a feathered accent, let animal features inspire you. Accent your bouquet with a touch of leopard print ribbon or carry a flower associated with an animal or named for a creature it resembles—the toad lily, tiger lily, spider lily, bat flower, parrot tulip, bird of paradise, or "wildcat" odontoglossum or "spider" arachnis orchid. Or enhance your exotic style with orchids—such as "moth" or "butterfly" phalaenopsis—that mimic insects in order to attract pollinators. Delphinium gets its name from the Latin word for "dolphin." Columbine, when pointed downward, resembles a group of doves. A carnivorous plant, such as the cobra lily, can reinforce an animal-themed bouquet.

Left: **CAMPBELL.** *Tiny toad lilies add a hint of color and funky shape.* 12-inch hand-tied bouquet of 'Anuschka' rose, toad lily (late summer–fall), longiflorum Asiatic hybrid lilies, fiddlehead fern, and colorful foliage, trimmed with ⅝-inch double-faced satin ribbon. ♦ ♦ ♦

Above: **PHALAENOPSIS ORCHID.** This orchid is nicknamed the "moth orchid."

BERNADETTE. *Leopard print on the handle accents a design suggested by animal markings.* 10-inch hand-tied bouquet of arachnis orchids, cobra lilies, mokara orchids, 'Camel' roses, fern curls, paphiopedilum orchids, carnations, and kangaroo paw, trimmed with double-faced satin accented with leopard-print stretch velvet ribbon. Gown: Saison Blanche, with vintage mink stole; earrings: Nadri. ♦♦♦

Left: **RAMONA**. *A deep-jade-green ribbon adds a luxurious and mysterious look to neutral-toned flowers.* 8-inch wired bouquet of 'Sahara' roses, mini cymbidium orchids, and arachnis orchids, trimmed with a 2-inch-wide silk double-faced satin ribbon. ♦♦

Above: **SKYLA**. *A butterfly-inspired creation.* 8-inch wired bouquet of mokara orchids and 'Terra Cotta' roses, trimmed with a 1½ -inch luminous taffeta ribbon. 1½-inch wired butterfly taffeta ribbon also shown. ♦♦

AN ORCHID COLLECTION. Orchids are some of the most intriguing flowers because many of them resemble beautiful winged insects. These are some of my favorite orchids for unique and modern insect-themed bouquets.

BEVERLY. *Post vintage buttons on fabric-coated wire that looks like thread.* 12-inch hand-tied bouquet of 'Antique Romantica' roses, 'Quatres Cortes' roses, freesia, and vintage buttons, trimmed with silk double-faced satin ribbon. Buy fabric-coated wire at a florist supply outlet. Gown and veil: Richard Glasgow. ♦♦♦♦

4

Something Borrowed: Inspiring Traditions

THE BRIDE TRADITIONALLY WEARS AN ITEM OF SENTIMENTAL VALUE—A FAMILY heirloom or something special from a woman she admires—and there are many lovely ways to incorporate such things into your bouquet. ❧ Wire buttons from your mother's wedding dress and make them part of your bouquet, or sew floral appliqués from her gown onto your bouquet ribbon. Tie an heirloom sixpence into the knots on a ribbon, wire a piece of a sister's jewelry and insert it among roses, or wrap a friend's bridal handkerchief around your bouquet stem. ❧ You can also "borrow" a style from the past. Choose a crocheted gown inspired by the bohemian style, or wear a sleek dress with a black sash and carry a bouquet inspired by new-wave or punk rock. ❧ Or gather a few special flowers for your bouquet from an old garden of a family member or friend. A few stems of double hellebore, pink muscari, or scented 'Armandii' clematis vines from the garden of someone close to you will make your bouquet charmingly unique.

FINDING BEAUTIFUL GARDEN FLOWERS

I'm nostalgic about a time when flowers were not grown in warehouses or imported from remote hills along the equator. Luckily, beautiful flowers are still found in private gardens or those of local specialty growers. Many sentimental favorites—camellias, rhododendrons, magnolias, clematis, azaleas, passion flower, foxgloves, hollyhocks, honeysuckle, sweet violets, bougainvillea, lamb's ear, clover, forget-me-nots, tree peonies—are not mass-produced as cut flowers. If you don't have your own garden, survey the flowers grown by family members, friends, or neighbors, or try other local sources. I love Seattle's Pike Place market, where farmers offer tulips, daffodils, sweet peas (with tendrils!), dahlias, buttercups, lupines, and lily varieties not produced by the large growers. Farmers' markets may also be a great source for unusual blooms. Or, with your florist, visit your local wholesale flower market, where you might find unusual garden lilacs, huge viburnum branches, cherry blossoms, or even buckets of herbs or branches collected from the woods.

Family Heirlooms

In some families, brides incorporate heirlooms—an embroidered handkerchief, a fancy brooch, a locket with special photos—into their bridal bouquets. Such traditional tokens, passed down from mother to daughter, can be wired and inserted among the flowers or be used in the wrapping on the handle. If your mother saved her gown but you are not wearing it, you might wrap the stems of your bouquet with a swatch of the fabric. Some brides carry a family bible, unadorned or decorated with a small cluster of flowers. If you don't have an heirloom, you can start your own tradition by including in your bouquet an item that can be passed down to future generations. One possibility: Create a family crest or monogram for the bouquet ribbon.

Left and above: **ELIZABETH.** *The rich colors of this wrist corsage were inspired by stained glass in a Gothic cathedral.* Corsage and hair piece of hydrangeas, cattleya orchids, and 'Merry Mac' dendrobium orchids. To make the bible's "bookmark," the flowers are wired, then tied into the knots of the several feet of trailing silk ribbon. Gown and veil: Madina Vadache. ♦

Left: **BOLD TRIM.** *A design with unexpected proportions—such as oversized ribbon with a small, clutch nosegay—can be charming.* Left: **PAIGE.** 9-inch hand-tied bouquet of 'Delilah' roses and heuchera leaves, trimmed with 4-inch double-faced satin ribbon. ♦♦ Right: **AIMEE.** 9-inch wired bouquet of hydrangeas and phalaenopsis orchids, trimmed with 5-inch wired French taffeta ribbon. It's easiest to find mauve hydrangeas in the fall. ♦♦♦

Right: **ROSALIND.** *A bride who may need a handkerchief can wrap it around the stem of her bouquet.* 10-inch hand-tied bouquet of 'Aqua' roses, hyacinths (late winter–spring), muscari (late winter–spring), and lamb's ear (spring–fall). Vintage handkerchief; monogram: Filigree Monograms. ♦♦♦

Vintage Looks

Today's fashion favors a vintage look. But how can that work with flowers, which should look fresh and flawless, with every petal exhibiting perfection? The truth is that it is sometimes aesthetically pleasing for a flower to be a little rough around the edges.

ANTIQUED AND DISTRESSED

Flowers grown outdoors, such as hydrangeas and garden roses, often look charming when slightly tattered by the elements. Even some flowers grown in a hothouse may exhibit an "antique" appearance. For instance, some orchids have been bred to have faded, mottled, "vintage-looking" striping.

If I am on the hunt for the perfect vintage look, I may "tweak" a flower—for example, spritzing a tiny amount of black cherry floral paint on taupe 'Sahara' roses to give them the sepia tone of an old photograph. Incorporating herbs is another way to give a bouquet an earthy, vintage look.

Some flowers—pansies, baby's breath, lavender—simply evoke the word "antique" and are pretty in tiny posy clutches. Pansies, with their casual, relaxed, "shabby chic" charm, look pretty tied with a silk ribbon that has been distressed with scissors (see page 31). Pansies generally aren't available on the cut flower market and need to be picked from a garden. I buy flats of them from my local nursery.

Left: **SYDNEY.** *Weather-distressed hydrangeas are like your favorite "worn" designer jeans. I love the weather spotting on these fall-harvested hydrangeas.* 12-inch hand-tied bouquet of "antiqued" hydrangeas (fall), 'Pullman Orient Express' roses, double pink lisianthus, and pincushion scabiosa (summer), trimmed with 1½-inch velvet ribbon. ♦ ♦ ♦

Right: **ODETTE.** *Pansies tied together can be quite dense, so I used mokara orchids as a base and to fill out this bouquet.* 6-inch hand-tied bouquet of baby's breath, pansies, and mokara orchids, trimmed with a silk shantung ribbon. These flowers are best in spring and fall. ♦

Different FLOWERS, SAME EFFECT

Top: **ANNETTE.** 6-inch wired posy of stephanotis spritzed with black cherry paint. ♦♦♦

Left: **AFTON.** 9-inch hand-tied bouquet of 'Sahara' roses and "antiqued" hydrangeas (fall). In winter, spring, and summer, use floral paint (available from retail florists) to "antique" white hydrangeas. ♦♦

Right: **LOLITA.** 8-inch hand-wired bouquet of 'Sahara' roses and phalaenopsis orchids. ♦♦♦

Your florist may not be able to find every flower you want, and you may have to make a last-minute decision or two. But no worries—you can get a very similar look using different flowers.

Downtown Mod

There is no reason why wedding bouquets cannot be hip and pretty at the same time. Just a touch of sassy flowers—mottled dahlias or two-tone gerbera daisies—complement a fun mod gown with tiered layers or an empire baby doll bodice with a tea length hemline. Playful syncopation of colors and shapes can deliver a taste of the unexpected. Funky bouquets can be designed using unexpected pairings, unconventional inserts, and jazzy colors. I add "mod" style to bouquets with multi-hued speckled dahlias, spray-painted pink stephanotis, vintage beaded flowers, bright ribbons, and unusual flowers like wired fuchsia blossoms. One of my favorite design elements is ribbon sewn to look like ribbon candy (see page 31 for how to do it).

Left: **TATUM.** *The oddest things can suggest a design! As I made this bouquet, I was thinking of 1960s wallpaper designs.* 12-inch hand-tied bouquet of dahlias (best summer–fall), sunflower gerbera daisies, statice, hydrangeas, craspedia, fern curls, mini calla lilies, and vintage beaded flowers, trimmed with 3-inch taffeta ribbon. ♦♦♦

Right: **BEATRIX.** *The garden flower fuchsia is very unusual in a bouquet. This one was inspired by a jazzy blues song I heard in a club.* 11-inch hand-tied bouquet of calla lilies, hydrangeas, 'Splendid Renate' pink roses, fuchsia blossoms (summer–fall), heather, and 'Marie Claire' butterscotch roses, trimmed with a 2-inch double-faced satin ribbon. *The wired fuchsia blossoms are delicate but will last through ceremony, photos, and reception. I kept them, fully misted, in a sealed plastic corsage container and added them to the bouquet just before handing it to the bride.* ♦♦♦

PHOEBE. 10-inch hand-tied bouquet of dahlias (best summer–fall), stephanotis, variegated lily grass, coleus (summer–fall), craspedia, 'Super Green' roses, and chinaberries, trimmed with 1½-inch grosgrain ribbon. Gown: Madina Vadache. ♦ ♦

Shape, pattern, AND COLOR ARE EQUALLY IMPORTANT TO THIS BOUQUET'S STYLE.

Boho Vintage

Borrowing from the bohemians is a fun way to bring a "retro" style into your wedding attire. For example, for a bride whose slinky knit crocheted gown went on over the head like a sweater, I designed a luxurious mix of yarn-like amaranthus, 'Black Baccara' roses, and gladiolus blossoms, and wrapped the stem with a yarn trim to accent the overall look.

CASSANDRA. *Hanging amaranthus, which looks like long locks of chenille, complements a crocheted gown.* 12-inch hand-tied bouquet of 'Black Baccara' roses, 'Super Green' roses, amaranthus (summer–fall), and gladioli, trimmed with double-faced satin and decorator fringe. Gown: Nicole Miller; headband: private collection; jewelry: Luly Yang Couture. ♦♦♦

High Style

Some brides prefer a casual feel for their ceremony, dress, and flowers, while others pull out all the stops and go for a particularly striking, elegant, or opulent look.

RED-CARPET GLAMOUR

A glamorous bouquet is about fantasy—imagine a glitzy gown and a riot of roses stealing the scene on the red carpet. Red roses, orchids, and oriental lilies are—bar none—the most glamorous flowers. Some of their colors are so beautiful that all they need is a velvet ribbon and matching lipstick. The 'Happy Hour,' my favorite red rose, has a velvety appearance and a perfectly round form.

Above: **RED AND WHITE ROSES.** Roses epitomize glamour. Here the contrast of red and white is beautifully softened by a delicate peach.

Right: **JACQUELINE.** *Lilies can be expensive, but just a few stems make a gorgeous bouquet. Trumpet lilies create a dramatic 1930s look with a slinky, columnar gown. 24-inch hand-tied, arm-held bouquet of 'Triumphator' trumpet lilies, 'Avalanche' roses, and philodendron leaves. Gown: Jenny Packham.* ♦♦♦

BRIGETTE. 10-inch hand-tied bouquet of 'Happy Hour' roses, trimmed with a 2-inch velour ribbon. Gown: Ines di Santo. ♦♦

Small details CAN MAKE A LOOK SPECIAL. HERE BEAUTIFUL RED PINS SECURE THE VELVET RIBBON, AND A BOW AT THE BOTTOM OF THE HANDLE LENDS A COUTURE TOUCH.

STELLA. *African native gloriosa lilies have an exotic "spider" shape. Their cranberry red and golden yellow highlights are perfect for the bride who accessorizes in gold.* 12-inch-wide spray, in designer foam, of gloriosa lilies, 'Porcelina' spray roses, 'Limona' roses, and cymbidium orchids, trimmed in a double-faced satin ribbon that has been ruffled (see page 31). ♦♦♦

THE ROYAL TOUCH

Create a royal look for your wedding by using elements of a queen's regalia, such as an embroidered purple gown and a jeweled coronet and scepter, reinterpreted with modern restraint. Instead of a full purple or blue gown trimmed with gold threads, for the ceremony you might wear a beautiful ivory-trimmed cropped jacket with a mock Elizabethan collar and then, for the reception, take it off to reveal a perfect beaded strapless evening gown. If you see yourself as more a princess than a queen, fashion a royal tiara out of flowers.

Your bouquet can be a royal scepter. The perfect source of royal purple or royal blue is the hydrangea. To complement and warmly set off magentas, I use orange shades of red. Another way to add a royal touch is to use flowers associated with royalty. The iris (fleur de lis) represented purity in the coat of arms of the French monarchy. Other "royal" flowers include Queen Anne's lace, red roses (emblems of English royal dynasties), the king protea, and the peony, often called "queen of the garden flowers."

Left: **EUNICE.** *Gold cord weaves through a mix of the feminine and the masculine—the tropical king protea and the queen of the garden flowers, the peony.* 12-inch hand-tied bouquet of king proteas, peonies (fall–spring), purple velvet, 'Camel' roses, and lilacs (spring). Purple velvet is generally available only as a cutting from a greenhouse plant. ♦♦♦

Center: **ISADORA.** *The expression "blue blood" means noble birth, and the distinct royal blue of the iris is perfect for a regal wedding.* 10-inch hand-tied bouquet of iris, cattleya orchids, and 'Splendid Renate' roses, trimmed with 2-inch dupioni silk ribbon. ♦♦

Right: **MAXINE.** *Common flowers make up this uncommon jewel-toned bouquet.* 10-inch hand-tied bouquet of delphinium, mini calla lilies, freesia, and 'Big Fun' roses, trimmed with 1¹/₂-inch taffeta ribbon in a simple spiral wrap. ♦♦

A round, NATURAL DOME SHAPE MAKES RICH, WARM COLORS EVEN MORE REGAL.

ADELINE. 12-inch hand-tied bouquet of hydrangeas, ranunculus (year-round, but best in spring and fall), double tulips, and 'Karadise' roses. Gown and jacket: Luly Yang Couture. ♦♦♦

Dancing on Air

In the early 1940s, when the world was at war, cut flowers were scarce and brides used more tulle than flowers in their bouquets. Many modern wedding gowns seem to have been inspired by these "ballerina" bouquets—if not by costumes from a classical ballet. Light, airy flowers look best with ballerina gowns. To match sheer, fluffy dresses made of tulle, silk chiffon, or organza, I use lightweight flowers, like orchids, trimmed with tulle, or a loose construction of sweet peas. For a lighter-than-air look, I like nerine or gloriosa lilies, or a round nosegay of wired 'Casablanca' oriental lilies. Feathers and tufts of tulle are pretty accents that lend an airy feel. The spray bouquet, popular in the early 1900s, is beautiful with a ballerina gown or any large ball-gown skirt made of French tulle. At outdoor weddings, the open design of a spray bouquet lets natural light flood in and illuminate each flower.

Left: **TATIANA.** *A compact nosegay can look light and airy when you add a tulle bow.* 9-inch wired bouquet of dendrobium orchids, phalaenopsis orchids, and hydrangeas, trimmed with 6-inch sage tulle ribbon. ♦♦

Above: **LUCA.** *Sweet peas rest on a cloud of tulle.* 10-inch hand-tied bouquet of sweet peas (spring–early summer). Tufts of 6-inch tulle that have been shirred surround the flowers. ♦

Opposite: **ROBYN.** 14-inch bouquet, in designer foam, of sweet peas, lily-of-the-valley, Angelique tulips, winter daphne, and lady's mantle (all most reliably available in spring), and plumosa fern (sprayed white to give the flowers a dusty gray backdrop). Gown: Vera Wang; necklace: Michal Negrin. ♦♦♦

At an outdoor wedding, BRIGHT LIGHT FILLS THE SPACE BETWEEN THE FLOWERS OF THIS SPRAY BOUQUET, LIGHTWEIGHT FOR ITS SIZE AND BEAUTIFULLY FRAGRANT.

MAKING THE GIOVANNA BOUQUET

This bouquet was inspired by a chic net veil, reminiscent of the veils attached to pillbox hats in the early twentieth century. Tiny circles of tulle surround individually wired blossoms and act as airy fillers between the flowers.

Step 1. Wire 1 large cymbidum orchid and 3 dendrobium orchids, then tape them together in a cluster. Make about 5 clusters. Also wire about 5 individual cymbidium orchids. (See pages 25 and 26 for instructions for wiring flowers.)

Step 2. To make the tulle bonnets, cut wide net tulle into 25 or 30 eight-inch squares. Take 8 or 10 of the squares at a time and poke the centers into your hand so that all the edges are sticking up. Feather or tatter the tulle by cutting randomly downward toward your hand. For a small stack of tulle, you will need to make at least 30 cuts. Pull off any excess pieces of cut tulle.

Step 3. Open the stack of tulle squares. Cut a tiny slit in the center of each square and slip two or three up the "stem" of each individually wired cymbidium. The tulle should hold in place if you cut a small enough slit. Tape the individual cymbidiums with tulle bonnets together with the clusters from step 1 to form the full bouquet. Use as much or as little tulle as you like. Colored tulle and a mix of colored cymbidium orchids can also be used to create a wide variety of looks. (See pages 25 and 26 for how to tape wired bouquets.)

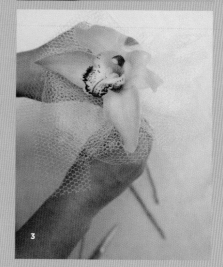

Tufts of tulle netting IN THE BOUQUET COMPLEMENT THE BRIDE'S CHIC LITTLE VEIL.

GIOVANNA. 8-inch wired bouquet of cymbidium orchids and dendrobium orchids, trimmed with a ribbon of cut and sheared tulle. Veil: Cicada Bridal. ♦♦

Trips Through Time

Styles from ancient to modern inspire floral sophistication, the luxury of using many types of blooms, and a striking, cutting-edge look.

NEOCLASSICAL ELEGANCE

Long, columnar gowns with height-enhancing details and flowers that stand proud, such as the calla lily or the French tulip, recall the elegance of times past. Shapely mermaid gowns and draping, cowl-backed dresses are all about silhouette, and to match them I love bouquet shapes that are long, lean, draping, and pretty enough to be carved in stone. You might include large acanthus leaves, the model for motifs atop classical Grecian columns or stems of papyrus that an ancient Egyptian queen might have carried.

ALEXANDRA. 20-inch-long, hand-tied arm bouquet of black podocarpus, French flame parrot tulips (spring), standard tulips, and gloriosa lilies, trimmed with double-faced satin ribbon. Gown: Le Sposa di Giò. ♦♦♦

A dress that is showy FROM ALL SIDES REQUIRES A BOUQUET
THAT COMPLEMENTS IT WHEN VIEWED FROM EVERY ANGLE.

Calla lilies ECHO THE CLASSIC LINES OF THE GOWN'S MERMAID SKIRT.

Left: **TARA**. 20-inch-tall arm bouquet of 'Green Goddess' calla lilies and 'Vermeer' calla lilies, trimmed with moiré taffeta ribbon. Gown: Ines di Santo. ♦♦♦

Right: **BLAIR**. *In ancient times, brides carried bouquets of wheat, a symbol of fertility. In summer, before it's ready for harvest, fresh wheat is a beautiful green.* 10-inch hand-tied bouquet of green wheat, trimmed with double-faced satin ribbon. Gown: Madina Vadache. ♦

BAROQUE STILL LIFE

Most personal gardens do not produce multiples of uniform flowers such as you would find in a commercial flower market. Because a typical garden offers an eclectic mix of blooms, it can be difficult to design an entire bouquet around one flower. This reality inspired me to design bouquets that a baroque-era still-life painter might have fashioned from flowers in his garden as a subject for a composition. I choose beautiful blooms, one each of several types of flowers, for these distinct ensembles of botanical treasures. "One of each" designs can be gorgeous if pulled together with a healthy dose of inspiration. "Borrowing" a variety of stems from the gardens of friends and family members makes a truly unique statement.

Left: **PRISCILLA.** *A baroque-era painter might have created this fantasy bouquet—late-summer chocolate sunflowers with early-summer peonies and exotic orchids.* 10-inch hand-tied bouquet of phalaenopsis orchids, cymbidium orchids, sunflowers, cattleya orchids, privet berry (late fall–early spring), and peonies (fall–spring), trimmed with double-faced satin ribbon. ♦♦♦

Above and opposite: **AMANDA.** 12-inch hand-tied bouquet of Dutch amaryllis (winter–spring), hypericum, three varieties of cymbidium orchids, phalaenopsis orchids, hyacinths (late winter–spring), andromeda (pieris; late winter–spring) and sweet peas (spring–early summer), trimmed with hand-pleated moiré taffeta and ruched organdy ribbon. Gown: Madina Vadache. ♦♦♦

Rich neutral colors BALANCE A WIDE MIX OF BLOSSOM SIZES AND TEXTURES, WHILE TINY CRYSTAL BEADS ON POSTS ADD LUXURIOUS DETAIL.

ANTONELLA. 10-inch hand-tied bouquet of China chrysanthemums, ranunculus (year-round, but best in spring and fall), "antiqued" hydrangeas (fall), 'Lollypop' roses, cymbidium orchids, and sweet peas (spring–early summer), trimmed with wired moiré taffeta ribbon. ♦♦

A dense mix of COLORS RECALLS THE GRAND ART OF THE BAROQUE PERIOD.

New Wave

Not every bride is a fairy-tale princess. If she is more of a punk-rock goddess, her bouquet ought to be as smashing and electrifying as her personal style. For such brides, anthuriums have a leather-like texture and are a perfect shade of punk-rock red. I might also use such flashy tropicals as red ostrich plume ginger, heliconia, or bird of paradise.

Left: **ZOIE.** *Placing glossy anthuriums atop furry castor bean pods creates an unusual and stunning look.* 14-inch-long, hand-tied cascade of castor beans (fall), anthuriums, and 'Eric Taberly' roses, trimmed with 5-inch wired taffeta ribbon. Gown: Madina Vadache. ♦♦♦

Right: **ROXANNE.** *An alternative look: Black ti leaves look like leather, creating a bold, edgy look with an asymmetrical gown.* 12-inch hand-tied bouquet of 'Akito' roses and ti leaves, trimmed with 2½-inch striped taffeta ribbon. Gown: Madina Vadache. ♦♦♦

East and West

Cultural heritage—the one you or your groom were born into or one that you admire—can be a creative jumping-off point for your bouquet design.

ASIAN MOTIFS

Many brides of Eastern heritage who have white weddings add splashes of oriental influence. Even if your background is not Asian, you may be inspired to design your bouquet with an East-meets-West flair. Many popular flowers—orchids, chrysanthemums, lilies, marigolds, peonies, lotus flowers, orchids, blooming fruit-tree branches—originated in the East and are part of the rich legacy of China, Japan, Southeast Asia, and India. Peonies, native to China, are a symbol of wealth, luck, and happiness. In Japan, purple is said to represent love. It makes a lovely color for a Japanese-themed bouquet.

Brides in many Eastern cultures don't carry a bouquet. Indian couples traditionally exchange long garlands of white and red flowers called jaimalas, though I have also seen Indian weddings in which a bride wearing a sari carries a traditional Western bouquet. Brides of Hawaiian heritage may wear a flower crown and haku lei (an open-ended garland of fragrant maile vines and white orchids), while the groom sports a lei of ti leaves.

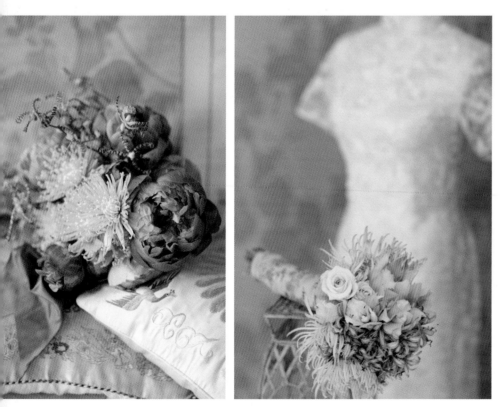

Left: **FENG.** *A Chinese watercolor painting inspired this bouquet.* 12-inch hand-tied bouquet of peonies (fall–spring), arachnis orchids, and spider chrysanthemums. ♦♦♦

Right: **MEILING.** *Gowns modeled on the Chinese qi pao—a short-sleeved, body-hugging dress with a tightly fitting stand-up collar—are often made from embroidered silk. I wrapped the bouquet's stem with this fabric.* 10-inch hand-tied bouquet of Shamrock mums, nerine lilies, cymbidium orchids, and 'Valerie' roses, trimmed with Chinese silk brocade fabric. Gown: Luly Yang Couture. ♦♦♦

Designed to match A PATTERNED RIBBON FROM A JAPANESE KIMONO.

MASUMI. 14-inch arm-held, hand-tied bouquet of 'Geisha' roses, vanda orchids, 'Sumatra' oriental lilies, and pink ostrich plume ginger, trimmed with 2-inch rayon ribbon. ♦♦♦

European and American Traditions

The bridal bouquet and formal "white wedding" are European and American cultural traditions that began in the nineteenth century. Queen Victoria was the archetypal Western bride, but traditions from other countries have also contributed style elements that today's brides can borrow. The guests at Norwegian and Dutch weddings plant lily-of-the-valley in a bride's garden after the ceremony for a symbolic annual "return of happiness." Fragrant flowers are customary for French wedding bouquets, and orange blossoms (a symbol of virginity) are popular with French and Spanish brides. A traditional Belgian bride carries, along with her flowers, a handkerchief with her name embroidered on it. Some English brides carry a horseshoe with ribbons, symbolizing good luck. Irish brides wear blue and carry bouquets containing English lavender, which symbolizes love and devotion. The bouquets on these pages are influenced by American country, French country, and Victorian English garden styles.

NANETTE. *In a Biedermeier bouquet, perfect, similar flowers are arranged tightly and in concentric rows. I prefer to make one that has subtle variation and slight imperfections.* 12-inch hand-tied bouquet of 'Juliette Drouet' roses, hydrangeas, English lavender, stephanotis, and purple oregano. Gown: Madina Vadache. ♦♦

Left: **MADISON**. *Inspired by a French salon.* 12-inch hand-tied bouquet of tulips, 'Rosita Vendela' roses, bells of Ireland, and veronica. ♦♦

Right, top: **BRITTANY**. *This bouquet recalls an afternoon in the English countryside.* 8-inch hand-wired bouquet of cymbidium orchids, 'Sweet Moments' roses, and artemesia, trimmed with 1½ -inch plaid wired taffeta ribbon. ♦♦

Right, bottom: **MICHELLE**. *Pink and green striped picot taffeta give this bouquet Parisian flair.* 8-inch wired bouquet of 'First Lady' roses and 'Mimi Eden' roses. Tiny bonnets of French ribbon surround the flowers. ♦♦

CHLOE. *Green-blue tones atop baby blue are lovely with this French blue dress. The spray design provides volume and depth without added weight.* 16-inch spray bouquet in 4 layers: on the bottom, assorted rich, specialty roses (early summer–fall), then a layer each of spiral eucalyptus and stephanotis; tweedia sprays over the top. Gown: Luly Yang Couture.

♦♦♦♦♦♦

5

Something Blue: Color in Bridal Fashion

COLOR AS STYLE—FROM A HINT OF PINK ON A SASH TO AN ENTIRE DRESS OF RED silk with a matching bouquet—is increasingly part of the modern bridal ensemble. The white dress is still predominant, but often it is accented with color in the bride's jewelry and flowers. Whether you will wear all-over color or just a touch, the color of your dress can be a starting point for the colors in your bouquet. ❧ Or a cherished memory might suggest the colors of your flowers. Did your fiancé give you peach roses when he proposed? Do you often think of the bright fuchsia orchids you saw on a wonderful trip to the tropics? Perhaps you want to carry the colors of your favorite rainbow sherbet ice cream. Choose colors that have special meaning for you, wherever they come from. ❧ Bouquet colors should work well with the bride's coloring—will her olive skin and brunette hair look best with warm shades of red or with cool, crisp whites? Then there are challenges offered by the setting—for example, how to make your favorite color, ripe orange, look formal with a grand ball gown in a dimly lit gilt ballroom. Flower colors take on different characters and moods and create unique effects depending on their shade, tone, and hue, as well as the shape and texture of the blooms. Choosing colorful flowers and coordinating them with your dress and accessories is all about reflecting who you are. The colors in your bouquet should match your personality and evoke your personal style.

A Spectrum of Sumptuous Color

I am a fanatic for color. Some floral designers suggest a limited palette of one or two colors. That approach can result in an elegant bouquet, but flowers are one area where you don't have to be restrained, and sometimes you can get the effect you want only by blending and contrasting many colors. Above all, have fun choosing the colors for your bouquet. Think about the flowers that catch your eye—interpret what they might say about you and, more important, what they mean to you.

BLUE (mysterious, composed, devoted, loyal, intuitive)

Associated with sky and sea, blue suggests divinity, mystery, and calm. A cool shade of blue is great for a bride who is collected and introspective, and deep blue is the color of faithfulness. Our world is framed in blue, but it is a rare color in the plant and animal kingdoms and is particularly uncommon, and prized, in flowers. Rare flowers like the blue Himalayan poppy hold mystery and wonder for flower enthusiasts. If you have a few precious stems of a delicate blue flower such as muscari or tweedia, combine it with ivory, white, or light yellow, as blue shows up beautifully adjacent to these colors. Adding a bit of blue-green or silver foliage helps maximize the impact of tiny blue flowers. For a bouquet with lots of blue flowers, go with hydrangea or delphinium blooms.

Left: **RACHEL.** *Blue flowers and blue earrings match the bride's bright blue eyes. The design was inspired by floral patterns on a teacup.* 10-inch hand-tied bouquet of 'Sunny Romantica' roses, 'Talea' roses, love-in-a-mist (nigella), muscari (late winter–spring), and nar-cissus (late winter–spring), trimmed with ³⁄₈-inch velvet ribbon. Gown: Ines di Santo; earrings: private collection. Another photo of the bouquet appears on page 43. ♦♦

Right: **MIRANDA.** *Juxtapose blue with purple for a peri-winkle effect.* 14-inch hand-tied bouquet of assorted hydrangeas (summer), blue lace scabiosa, and nigella "love-in-a-mist," trimmed with silk ribbon. ♦♦

ASHLYN. *A light dusting of turquoise flowwer paint gives green carnations a bluish glow.* 8-inch hand-tied bouquet of green carnations, bumblebee ornithogalums, dusty miller, artemesia, heather, and sea holly, trimmed with turquoise rayon fabric ribbon. Brooch: Jewels by Cara Couture Accessories. ♦♦♦

RED (playful, confident, audacious, remarkable, illustrious)

Red creates a spark. Evoking fire, zeal, and passion, this color of true love is associated with people who are fun-loving and intuitive. It's hard to ignore the bold contrast of a red bouquet against a white dress. For simpler, more austere styles, a deep shade works best. If you accessorize in red, keep it simple—a single red pendant on a necklace or a headband of red velvet. Red shoes are a more restrained expression; hidden under your skirt during the ceremony, they will be seen by all when you dance at the reception.

There are many shades of red, and the hue and intensity should be right for your gown. I like to match bright bluish-red flowers with off-white or bright white dresses. Eggshell-colored gowns look luxurious with red-orange or a red-blue, as long as the color is deep and velvety. An ivory or champagne gown looks beautiful with rusty reds. Roses are an obvious choice for a bride who wants red in her bouquet. More unusual red flowers include amaryllis in winter, tulips in winter and spring, and poppies in summer.

Left: **VANESSA.** *This casual bouquet, with a touch of blue added for interest, would be pretty in a country wedding.* 12-inch hand-tied bouquet of 'Ranuncula' roses, muscari (late winter–spring), ostrich plume ginger, dahlias (best summer–fall), flame parrot tulips (spring), and amaranthus (summer–fall). ♦♦♦

Right: **HALLE.** *If you can't find red pearl pins, use red nail polish to paint pearls added to wired stephanotis—as well as the bride's fingernails.* 16-inch-long hand-tied arm bouquet of 'Red Intuition' roses and stephanotis, trimmed with wired, double-faced satin ribbon. ♦♦♦

BETSY. *Sassy red shoes, worn under two petticoat layers, are this bride's fun little secret.* 10-inch hand-tied bouquet of "antiqued" hydrangeas (fall), 'Annabelle' hydrangeas (summer–fall), green carnations, "Kermit pom-pom" chrysanthemums, red viburnum, faux red berries, and tuberous begonias, trimmed with giant red rickrack sewn on 2-inch double-faced satin ribbon. Gown: Avioanni; shoes: Donna Karan. ♦♦

PINK (graceful, charming, coy, dainty, scrupulous, demure)

Associated with gentility and feminine grace, pink is popular for the sweet, blushing bride, but that hasn't always been the case. When I first started designing wedding bouquets, pink was stigmatized as saccharine and devoid of substance—it was not to be taken seriously. But recent fashion trends have favored it, and brides now use many of the widely varying shades of pink, including mauves, rose-pink, and coral. The unabashed femininity of pink makes it the perfect color for a bride.

FARRAH. *The 5-inch ribbon sash on the dress brings out subtle pink peonies in the background of this crisp, clean, classic bouquet.* 14-inch hand-tied bouquet of 'Xotica' oriental lilies, cattleya orchids, and peonies (fall–spring), trimmed with taffeta ribbon that matches the bride's sash. Gown: Amy Kuschel; ribbon sash: romanticribbons.com; necklace: vintage milk glass, private collection. ♦♦♦

This bouquet, ITS TINY FLOWERS ALL HAND-WIRED,
IS LIKE A GIANT PIECE OF FASHION MILLENARY.

KYLA: The 5-inch ribbon sash on the dress brings out subtle pink peonies in the background of this crisp, clean, classic bouquet. 24-inch wired cascade of hyacinths (late winter-spring), 'Bianca Candy' roses, dendrobium orchids, stephanotis, and mini tulle millenary flowers. Gown: Madina Vadache; necklace: Michal Negrin. ♦♦♦♦♦

NAOMI. *The bride's dress, her hair flowers, and the bouquet's foliage collar are celadon green, yet lavender dominates.* 13-inch hand-tied, domed bouquet of 'Bluebird' roses, 'Mari Romantica' roses, 'Annabelle' hydrangeas (summer–fall), "Popcorn" ('Ayesha') hydrangeas (summer–fall), bumblebee ornithogalums, chrysanthemums, and geranium leaves, trimmed with double-faced satin ribbon. Gown and hair flower: Luly Yang Couture. ♦♦♦

LAVENDER (sensitive, noble, discerning, wistful, creative)

Deep shades of purple are opulent and passionate; tinted to a lighter shade, lavender feels more sensitive. Lavender is utterly romantic—lilacs of this color represent first love, roses love at first sight. A mix of pink and blue, lavender contains qualities of both. It can be overshadowed by other colors, but mixing it with shades of mint and celadon green allow it to dominate. Lavender also shows up well with butter yellow, and a mauve (orchid) shade of lavender looks great with taupe and brown. To make lavender stand out on its own, use a backdrop of white, ivory, or green.

An excellent accent, lavender complements just about all colors. I sometimes use it as a filler between blue flowers (blue is the rarest color for flowers). When blue is paired with purple, the two blend to make the eye see periwinkle. I have made many bouquets using lavender as just one component—tropical schemes with purple, pink, and yellow, and rich, jewel-tone palates featuring blues and reds.

Left: **ISABELLA**. *Being surrounded with rosettes, including a silk rose, is an extremely romantic look.* 14-inch hand-tied bouquet of peonies (fall–spring), kale, and 'Pacific Blue' roses. Gown: Valentino; necklace: Two's Company, with added silk rose. ♦♦♦

Right: **LANI**. *This bouquet is beautifully sweet-scented—fruity hyacinth with the soft, tropical aroma of stephanotis.* 10-inch hand-tied bouquet of hyacinths (late winter–spring), stephanotis, and plumosa fern (sprayed with white paint to become a silvery gray). ♦♦♦

GREEN (generous, benevolent, humble, gentle, trusting)

The most pleasant of colors and one the eye always welcomes, green is the color of foliage and thus of abundance and renewal. Its gentle quality is lovely with any shade of white wedding gown. Many white and yellow flowers have a lot of green in them as well. Magnetic shades of lemon-lime and apple green are found in orchids, roses, ranunculus, chinaberries, viburnums, and many more.

Above, left: **THEA.** *The mix of green and black is so chic and modern.* 8-inch wired bouquet of green cymbidium orchids and ti leaves, trimmed with a 1-inch silk ribbon. ♦♦

Above, right: **MARILYN.** *Wire tendrils are fun accents.* 12-inch hand-tied bouquet of 'Jade' roses and blue lace scabiosa, trimmed with ⅜-inch grosgrain ribbon sewn onto 5-inch wired taffeta. To form wire tendrils, wrap green wire around a bamboo skewer; slide out the skewers, cut the tendrils into short sprig clusters, mount them on wire, and insert them among the flowers. ♦♦♦

Opposite: **NERISSA.** *Cool shades of lemon and lime make me think of a sea nymph.* Crown and 10-inch hand-tied bouquet of phalaenopsis orchids, green muscari (late winter–spring), reindeer moss, and string of beads (senecio), with jade, ceramic, and crochet-covered bead accents. Gown: Pronovias. ♦♦♦♦

YELLOW (delightful, radiant, debonair, magnificent)

Associated with sunshine, optimism, energy, happiness, and peace, yellow can be simultaneously stimulating and mellow. Soft, buttery yellows complement many skin tones and look beautiful with ivory gowns. Brides who love this color can choose from flowers with happy shapes like sunflowers, daffodils, and gerbera daisies. The center of the daisy is also a beautiful and charming yellow. Roses grow in many shades of yellow, from soft, pastel shades to radiant gold, and forsythia and saffron-colored marigolds can make stunning yellow bouquets.

Left: **SUNDAY.** *Golds and grays combined with soft textures make for a cool, relaxed style.* 11-inch hand-tied bouquet of hydrangeas, paperwhites, white spray roses, double tulips, acacia (mimosa; winter–spring), and dusty miller, trimmed with 2-inch silk dupioni ribbon with applied trim. ♦♦

Center: **KAILEY.** *A pinch of coral pink in sunshine yellow creates unexpected excitement.* 11-inch hand-tied bouquet of camellias (spring), 'Citronella' roses, daffodils (late winter–spring), dahlias (best summer–fall), 'Primrose' lilacs (spring), and yellow jasmine. Monogram: Filigree Monograms. ♦♦♦

Right: **ALEXIS.** *Bright white and yellow are crisp and clean.* 10-inch hand-tied bouquet of 'Yellow Island' roses, nerine lilies, mini calla lilies, and beaded flowers. A piece of the gown's fabric embellished with pearls wraps the stem. ♦♦

Maize yellow roses BRING OUT THE GOWN'S RICH IVORY COLOR.

ADDISON. 12-inch hand-tied bouquet of 'Limona' roses and stephanotis on the vine. Gown and veil: Elie Saab. ♦♦♦♦

ORANGE (vivacious, dynamic, gregarious)

The most energizing color, orange lights up in many different contexts. Carrying orange flowers expresses a keen sense of style, and when a bride with cinnamon-red hair and fair skin holds an orange bouquet, the effect is gorgeous. Orange stands out even in a room full of flowers but comes across as exuberant rather than boastful. When orange is mixed with yellow, as in pretty roses like 'Sari' or 'Milva,' it has a delicious quality. Orange can range from the spicy rusty tones of flame calla lilies to the crisp, fresh tangerine found in tulips or sandersonia. Associated with autumn and popular with fall brides, orange is also a great choice for a bright summer garden wedding—it holds up well to sunlight and doesn't get washed out.

Left: **JOVIE.** *Salmon zinnias are complemented by ruffled kale in a very pretty, deep shade of seafoam green.* 10-inch hand-tied bouquet of salmon zinnias (summer), 'Sahara' roses, celosia (late summer–fall), and kale, trimmed with peach taffeta ribbon. Gown: Madina Vadache. ♦

Right: **CHARLOTTE.** *A sumptuous mix of flowers to match the bride's purse.* 12-inch hand-tied bouquet of beehive ginger, rhododendrons (spring), 'Naranja' roses, daffodils (late winter–spring), and heuchera leaves, trimmed with velvet and checked taffeta ribbons. Purse: Inge Christopher. ♦♦♦

EVANGELINE. *Coral peonies are a favorite of mine. Coral complements many skin tones and is a great choice for just about any bride.* 12-inch hand-tied bouquet of 'Milva' roses, peonies (fall–spring), and wax flowers, trimmed with 1½-inch velvet ribbon. Brooch: vintage. ♦♦

Left: **KINETA**. *A cuff of fabric sets off these beautiful two-toned roses.* 8-inch hand-tied bouquet of 'Cherry Brandy' roses, trimmed with a flower sleeve of fabric by Amy Butler, purchased at Pacific Fabrics & Crafts. ♦♦

Right: **SUMMER**. *A mix of orange shades and chocolate brown is both beautiful and modern.* 14-inch long, hand-tied arm bouquet of 'Movie Star' roses, mokara orchids, and ti leaves, trimmed with jacquard on ruffled double-faced satin ribbon. Gown: Carmela Sutera. ♦♦

BROWN (sensible, discreet, sophisticated, steadfast, reserved, dignified)

Brown's proper name is dark orange, yet it has a life of its own due to its associations with some of the most sensuous things we know—chocolate, coffee, rich top soil. The color brown stands out best when it is adjacent to a bright color. On its own, brown is very flattering when a bride wears a rum pink, toffee, beige, or creamy gown. Deep sepias, rusts, khakis, and burgundies are all part of the wide spectrum of colors we call brown.

Left: **CORINA.** *Waxy anthuriums are shaped like hearts. Their brown looks great when simply adorned with an apricot-gold ribbon.* 36-inch-long (with stems) hand-tied bouquet of 'Choco' anthuriums, trimmed with moiré taffeta ribbon. Gown: Elizabeth Fillmore. ♦♦

Right: **ARIA.** *If azaleas are not available, substitute orchids, and use smoke bush instead of dark euphorbia.* 10-inch hand-tied bouquet of hydrangeas, azaleas (spring), 'Camel' roses, echinacea (coneflower) pods, dark euphorbia (spring), and chocolate geranium leaves, trimmed with "French roast" silk-satin ribbon. ♦♦

Sherry-brown blooms MATCH TAUPE, & 'SHERRY BABY'
ORCHIDS DELICATELY WAFT CHOCOLATE.

Opposite: **NICOLE**. 30-inch-long (with greenery) arm cascade of oncidium orchids, 'Sherry Baby' orchids, cymbidium orchids, winterbud, and 'Armandii' clematis (spring–summer), trimmed with double-faced satin ribbon accented with cotton lace. Gown: Pronovias. ♦♦♦

Above: **KENDALL**. *Deep cinnamon-colored cymbidiums are gorgeous with velvet ribbon.* 8-inch wired bouquet of cymbidium orchids, fern curls, 'Sahara' roses, green muscari (best in spring), and preserved fan fern, trimmed with 1½ -inch velvet ribbon; champagne pearl pins are inserted up the stem. ♦♦

BLACK (serious, elegant, polished, dramatic, distinguished)

Occasionally a serious, elegant, dramatic, or spirited bride wants to add a bit of black to her ensemble. Black bridal accessories might include some (but not all!) of the following: black beading on the dress, a black outdoor cape, black opera gloves, a black sash, a black crystal and onyx necklace. Black flowers are rare, but very deep shades of purple and burgundy will create a "black" effect. Some flowers, like anemones and ornithogalums, have black centers that contrast with white petals. If you don't want black flowers but would like some black in your bouquet, you might tie light ivory flowers with a black ribbon.

Left: **ADRIENNE.** *When dark red flowers are paired with black privet berries and black ribbon, the colors will look black in low light.* 12-inch hand-tied bouquet of 'Black Baccara' roses, peonies (fall–spring), and privet berries (late fall–early spring), trimmed with 5-inch wired taffeta ribbon. ♦♦♦

Right: **CIARA.** *Black flowers beautifully complement the oyster-colored gown worn by a dark-haired bride. A black stole—or necklace or piece of jewelry—pulls the look together.* 10-inch hand-tied bouquet of blackish mini calla lilies and specialty parrot tulips (spring), trimmed with 2-inch silk dupioni ribbon. Shawl: Anne Klein; gown: Vera Wang. ♦♦♦

WHITE (pure-hearted, fresh, sublime)

You can never go wrong with a classic white wedding bouquet. Associated with perfection and purity, white is not really a color. Rather, it is a reflection of all colors—in other words, white is the color of light itself. The white rose, white lily, and white carnation are symbols of innocence, just as the white lily-of-the-valley is a symbol of hope, luck, and friendship. The white lilac represents family, the white dahlia the qualities of appreciation and respect. Soft-shaded white peonies, with their cup-shaped blossoms, suggest caring and protection. The brightest white bridal flowers include the gardenia, the stephanotis, the phalaenopsis orchid, and the oriental lily. If you want to carry white flowers, make sure to give your florist a swatch of your gown fabric; most white flowers are not pure white but have a touch of champagne, ivory, or even green.

Left: **THE CHARM OF A SMALL BOUQUET.** *One of the nice things about a small, hand-tied bouquet is that the bride can set it in a water glass at the table.* Left: **CATALINA.** Mini calla lilies. ♦♦ Right: **AGNES.** Simple, elegant white lily-of-the valley (in spring, widely available and half the out-of-season price) ♦♦ out of season; ♦ in season.

Right: **WHITLEY.** *A delicate piece of lace trim ties together the black centers of the anemones with the lacy texture of the lilacs.* 12-inch hand-tied bouquet of lilacs (spring), anemones (fall–spring), and hydrangeas. The stem is wrapped with 2¾-inch wide white double-faced satin with a piece of lace trim (available at fabric stores) over it. ♦♦♦

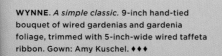

WYNNE. *A simple classic.* 9-inch hand-tied
bouquet of wired gardenias and gardenia
foliage, trimmed with 5-inch-wide wired taffeta
ribbon. Gown: Amy Kuschel. ♦♦♦

GABRIELLA. 14-inch hand-tied bouquet of hydrangeas, peonies (fall–spring), and stephanotis. This large dome bouquet is proportional to the skirt's size but allows bodice and skirt details to be seen. Gown: Elie Saab. ♦♦♦

White without greenery AGAINST A NATURAL WHITE SILK GOWN—SUBLIME.

Hot and Radiant

Bright, warmly colored wedding bouquets look spectacular at night as well as during the day. Cinnamon orange, flame red, marigold yellow, and hot pink are colors of excitement and fun. A bouquet using them is perfect for a hot August wedding or one that takes place in the fall, when nature shows off its most dramatic colors.

I love to juxtapose colors. Hot hues can be cooled with a touch of dark green, energized with chartreuse, or muted with a little dark purple or burgundy. Adding blue or white makes radiant colors look even brighter. It's always pleasing to mix warm color tones. I call warm colors mixed with green "fruit salad" colors. When I mix them with purples they are "jewel tones."

Sunny Romantica

Razzle Dazzle

Sanaa

Razzle Dazzle

Alabrahma

Riverdale

Above: **JEWEL TONE ROSES.** Vibrant and gorgeous, jewel tones are especially so in darker settings where magenta pinks, spicy reds, oranges, and golden yellows acquire a glow. Fair-skinned and fair-haired brides beware: Jewel tones may make you look "washed out."

Right: **LARISSA.** *Each leaf is wired before tying it into the bouquet.* 12-inch hand-tied bouquet of 'Riverdale,' 'Milva,' 'Sweet Moments,' 'Splendid Renate,' and 'Coup Soleil' roses, and croton leaves. Each leaf is wired before being tied into the bouquet. ♦♦♦

Above: **DOMANI.** *The stem wrap on a presentation arm bouquet can be as fancy as you want. Here tiny repeating bows echo the flowers' spiky shape.* 12-inch hand-tied bouquet of nerine lilies and 'Volata' amaryllis (winter–spring), trimmed with double-faced satin ribbon. ◆◆◆

Right: **BONITA.** *Deep chevrons cut in various lengths of ribbon echo the repeating V in the gown design.* 24-inch garland bouquet of 'Circus' roses, 'Tenga Venga' roses, and nerine lilies, trimmed with several streamers of 2¾-inch double-faced satin ribbon. Gown: Elizabeth Fillmore. ◆◆◆◆

Cool and Icy

A bride's bright white dress appears to glow when she carries cool-toned flowers. Cool colors—silvery gray, lavender, aqua blue, icy pink, minty green, greenish-white, shades of canary yellow—are mysterious and slightly detached. A cool color does not have to be a light shade or pastel. Enigmatic, dark shades of cool colors like plum (dark purple with a little blue) or wine burgundy (deep red with a touch of blue) nicely complement bright white. Cool colors, perfect in late winter or spring when crisply textured tulips and daffodils are in season, are also popular for beach weddings.

Left: **VIVIANNE.** *Shades of icy blue and cool lavender make a beautiful winter bouquet.* 10-inch hand-tied bouquet of hyacinths (late winter–spring) and Colorado spruce, trimmed with 5-inch wired taffeta ribbon. ♦♦

Center: **KARINA.** *Without the ribbon, this bouquet would have a lemon-lime tone. The cooling mint-green lends it a crisp feel.* 9-inch hand-tied bouquet of Weber's parrot tulips (spring), stephanotis, and paphiopedilum (lady's slipper) orchids, trimmed with 2-inch, mint-green, double-faced satin ribbon. Keep tulips out of light and in refrigeration (at 36 degrees Fahrenheit) the night before the ceremony so that they stay closed. Gown: Carmela Sutera. ♦♦

Right: **STACY.** *Dogwood is the central flower, but mint accents give this bouquet an icy edge.* 11-inch hand-tied bouquet of dogwood (spring), lily-of-the-valley (spring), lichen, and 'Avalanche' roses. The flowers are accompanied by little celadon stones on wires and wire wrapped with yarn curlicues. The wrap is made of ruffled decorator trim purchased at JoAnn Fabrics. ♦♦

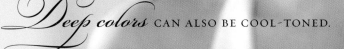

Deep colors CAN ALSO BE COOL-TONED.

NATASHA. 10-inch hand-tied bouquet of hellebore (best late fall–early spring), eucalyptus pods (fall–winter), muscari (late winter–spring), and purple pincushion (isopogon; winter–spring), trimmed with 2-inch, plum-colored velour ribbon. Gown: Sally Crew; fur bolero: Cassini. ♦♦

A Charmed Bouquet Toss

At a typical wedding reception, eligible bridesmaids and other single women line up to catch the bride's bouquet. Superstition says that the one who does so will be the next to marry. I like to combine the bouquet toss with an older tradition, the Victorian charm pull—from atop the cake, the eligible women pulled ribbons tied to charms that carried predictions.

I create tiny bouquets that sit on the cake, each tied to a charm and a fortune. A frog prince charm might accompany the saying "You will marry a dashing heartthrob," and an electric guitar charm might say, "You will marry a rock star." When the bride tosses these charming bouquets, each bachelorette receives a floral souvenir and a peek into her future. And the bouquet toss keeps the wedding bouquet intact for the bride who wants to preserve her flowers.

Left and opposite: **FORTUNA.** *Getting ready to toss a little posy to the bachelorettes.* Necklace: Michal Negrin; earrings and bracelet: Betsey Johnson.

Right: Tiny fortunes and charms are tied to each posy.

Preserving Your Wedding Bouquet

Cut flowers are ephemeral, but many brides preserve their wedding bouquet as a beautiful keepsake. There are two types of professional preservation: heating flowers and then vacuuming out all the moisture; and freeze-drying them. Both of these methods require specialized machines, which add significantly to the cost of preserving a bouquet professionally, as compared to doing it yourself (described below).

Professionally preserved flowers retain their shape and some of their color, and professionals can tint the preserved blooms to a color similar to when they were fresh. Most flowers can be preserved—a notable exception is the chrysanthemum, which tends to shatter when dried. Some flowers with high water content (orchids, lilies, stephanotis) can be preserved with freeze drying (the method usually used for these flowers), though they will be quite delicate; heating/vacuum method may be a better method. Preserved flowers won't last forever, but they can be a long-lasting keepsake that you will enjoy for many, many years.

The cost of professional flower preservation depends on the size of the bouquet. For a 12-inch dome bouquet of roses, you may spend as much on just the freeze-drying, shadow-boxing, and framing as you did on the fresh bouquet. Consult with a preservationist to get a quote.

You can also preserve your flowers yourself. (Note, however, that there is no fail-safe way to preserve flowers on your own, and that home techniques do not result in long-lasting preserved flowers.) Not many flowers can be air-dried. Those with lower water content—roses, hydrangeas, larkspur, statice—air-dry best.

Do-it-yourself preservation can be as simple as air-drying (hanging the flowers upside down in a dark, dry closet) or suspending them in a box of silica gel that you buy at a craft store. Some flowers that have a low water content and are naturally flat, like hydrangeas, daisies,w or violets, can also be pressed. Place the blossoms between heavy absorbent papers in a flower press, then glue the pressed flowers onto paper or between sheets of glass. I'd recommend that only experienced do-it-yourselfers try this method. Professionals can also press your flowers.

Preserved flowers must be protected from light, dust, and moisture. A glass enclosure is a good way to do this. It is best to use UV glass, which slows the fading of colors; shadow boxes made of UV glass are available at craft stores. There are many other charming ways to display your dried bouquet—in a vintage mini green-house or terrarium, under a glass garden cloche, or in an apothecary jar. Regular glass, which will not protect flowers from fading as well as UV glass, will keep dust and some moisture away from the preserved blossoms.

If you plan to have your bouquet professionally preserved, make the arrangements several weeks in advance. Your florist or wedding coordinator will likely know of someone in your area who preserves flowers and can assist you in handling the bouquet and preparing it for preservation. Be sure to tell your florist that you will preserve your bouquet so that you can choose flowers that are good candidates for preservation.

Top: **SHOWCASING A FREEZE-DRIED BOUQUET.** The Mimi bouquet from page 38, freeze-dried, tinted, and shadow-boxed in a vintage mini greenhouse. The petals retain their original shape. The rose is a great flower to freeze-dry. Freeze-dried by: Simone Perry of Timeless Garden.

Bottom: **AIR-DRIED YELLOW ROSES.** The bouquet at the left has been air-dried for several weeks and placed under a glass cloche. The fresh bouquet is shown at right. Air-dried flowers do not last as long and are much more brittle than freeze-dried flowers.

Flower Names

The list below gives the Latin (scientific) names for the flowers mentioned in this book. Capitalized Latin words are genus names (a genus contains one or more species). Two-part Latin names are species names. These names can help when you or your florist are ordering flowers, especially from abroad.

Common nicknames are given in lower case and double quotes—for example, Gardenia / "cape jasmine" (*Gardenia jasminoides*). Variety names are in single quotes or noted with the abbreviation "var." For flowers with many varieties (also known as cultivars), the names appear in a list under the flower name.

ACACIA / "MIMOSA" / "WATTLE"
(*Acacia baileyana*)
ACANTHUS (*Acanthus mollis*)
ACUBA LEAVES (*Aucuba japonica*)
ALLIUM (*Allium sphaerocephalon* 'Hair')
AMARANTHUS (*Amaranthus*)
    Hanging (*Amaranthus caudatus*)
    Upright (*Amaranthus hypochondriacus*)
AMARYLLIS
    'Volata' (*Amaryllis belladonna* 'Volata')
    'Naked Lady' (*Amaryllis belladonna* 'Naked Lady')
    Dutch amaryllis (*Hippeastrum* hybrid cultivars)
ANDROMEDA (*Pieris japonica*)
ANEMONE / "WINDFLOWER" (*Anemone*)
    Dutch (*Anemone coronaria*)
    Japanese (*Anemone hupehensis* var. *Japonica*)
ANTHURIUM / "FLAMINGO FLOWER"
(*Anthurium andreanum*)
    'Choco'
    Tulip (*Anthurium amnicola*)
ARTEMISIA (*Artemisia*)
    'Silver Queen'
ARTICHOKE / "GLOBE ARTICHOKE"
(*Cynara scolymus*)
ASCLEPIAS / "BUTTERFLY WEED"
(*Asclepias tuberosa*)
ASTILBE (*Astilbe arendsii*)
ASTRANTIA (*Astrantia major*)
AURICULA PRIMROSE (*Primula auricula*)
AZALEA (*Rhododendron augustinii*)
BABY'S BREATH (*Gypsophyila paniculata*)
    'Million Star'
BAT FLOWER (*Tacca chantrieri*)
BAY LEAF / "LAUREL LEAF" (*Laurus nobilis*)
BEGONIA (*Begonia*)
    Tuberous
    Rex begonia (*Begonia rexcultorum* hybrid)

BELLS OF IRELAND (*Molucella laevis*)
BERGENIA (*Bergenia*)
BERZELIA / "BAUBLES" (*Berzelia galpinii*)
BIRD OF PARADISE (*Streptocarpus*)
BLACKBERRY (*Rubus*)
BLUSHING BRIDE (*Serruria florida*)
BORONIA (*Boronia megastigma*)
BOUGAINVILLEA (*Bougainvillea glabra*)
BOUVARDIA (*Bouvardia longiflora*)
BRUNIA (*Brunia albiflora*)
BUPLEURUM (*Bupleurum griffithiii*)
BUTTERCUP (*Ranunculus ficaria*)
CAMELLIA (*Camellia*)
    'Debutante' (*Camellia japonica* 'Debutante')
    'Scentsation' (*Camellia japonica* 'Scentsation')
CALENDULA (*Calendula officinalis*)
CALLA LILY / "ARUM LILY"
(*Zantedeschia aethiopica*)
    'Green Goddess'
    Mini (*Zantedeschia* hybrid cultivars)
    'Vermeer' (*Zantedeschia* hybrid cultivars)
CARNATION (*Dianthus caryophyllus*)
CASTOR BEAN (*Ricinus communis*)
CELOSIA (*Celosia*)
    Bombay (*Celosia cristata*)
    Flame (*Celosia argentea*)
CHERRY BLOSSOM (*Prunus*)
CHINABERRY (*Melia azedarach*)
CHINA MUM (*Chrysanthemum grandiflorum*)
CHOCOLATE VINE (*Akebia quinata* 'Purple
Bouquet')
CHRYSANTHEMUM (*Chrysanthemum*)
    "Kermit pom-pom" (*Chrysanthemum x grandiflorum*
    Pom Pom 'Kermit')
    Shamrock (*Chrysanthumum x grandiflorum* 'Shamrock')
CLEMATIS (*Clematis*)
    Armandii (*Clematis armandii*)

CLOVER (*Trifolium*)
COBRA LILY (*Sarracenia*)
COLEUS (*Solenostemon*)
COLORADO SPRUCE (*Picea pungens*)
COLUMBINE (*Aquilegia*)
COSMOS (*Cosmos*)
    Chocolate (*Cosmos atrosanguineus*)
CRASPEDIA (*Craspedia globosa*)
CROTON LEAF (*Codiaeum variegatum*)
CURCUMA / "SIAM TULIP" (*Curcuma
alismatifolia*)
DURLY WILLOW (*Salix matsudana* 'Tortuosa')
DAFFODIL (*Narcissus*)
DAHLIA (*Dahlia*)
    Pompon
DELPHINIUM (*Delphinium*)
    Belladonna (*Delphinium belladonna*)
DOGWOOD (*Cornus*)
DUSTY MILLER (*Senecio cineraria*)
ECHEVERIA (*Echeveria*)
ECHINACEA / "CONEFLOWER" (*Echinacea*)
ENGLISH LAVENDER (*Lavandula angustifolia*)
EUCALYPTUS (*Eucalyptus*)
    Pod / "blue gum" (*Eucalyptus globules*)
    Seeded (*Eucalyptus polyanthemos*)
    Spiral (*Eucalyptus gunnii*)
EUCHARIS LILY / "AMAZON LILY"
(*Eucharis amazonica*)
EUPHORBIA (*Euphorbia*)
FERN
    Fan (*Adiantum aleuticum*)
    Fiddlehead / "black fiddle fern"
FEVERFEW, DAISY (*Tanacetum parthenium*)
FORGET-ME-NOT (*Myosotis*)
FORSYTHIA (*Forsythia*)
FOXGLOVE (*Digitalis*)

FREESIA (*Freesia*)

FRENCH TULIP (*Tulipa*)

FRITILLARIA / "SNAKE'S HEAD" (*Fritillaria meleagris*)

FUCHSIA (*Fuchsia* hybrids)

GARDENIA / "CAPE JASMINE" (*Gardenia jasminoides*)

GERBERA DAISY (*Gerbera jamesonii*)

GENISTA / "EASTER BROOM" (*Genista*)

GERANIUM (*Pelargonium*)
    Chocolate-scented (*Pelargonium tomentosum x 'Chocolate'*)
    Scented (*Pelargonium graveolens 'Old Rose'*)

GINGER (flowers of many genera are nicknamed "ginger")
    Beehive (*Zingiber spectabile*)
    Ostrich plume (*Alpinia purpurata*)

GLADIOLUS (*Gladiolus*)

GLORIOSA LILY (*Gloriosa superba*)

GREEN WHEAT (*Triticum*)

HEATHER (*Erica*)

HELIOTROPE (*Heliotrope arborescens*)

HELLEBORE (*Helleborus*)

HELICONIA (*Heliconia*)

HEUCHERA (*Heuchera*)

HOLLYHOCK (*Alcea rosea*)

HONEYSUCKLE (*Lonicera*)

HOSTA (*Hosta*)

HYACINTH (*Hyacinth orientalis*)

HYDRANGEA (*Hydrangea*)
    'Annabelle' (*Hydrangea arborescens*)
    Common (*Hydrangea macrophylla*)
    Lacecap (*Hydrangea serrata*)
    Pee Gee (*Hydrangea paniculata 'Grandiflora'*)
    "Popcorn" (*Hydrangea macrophylla 'Ayesha'*)

HYPERICUM (*Hypericum androsaemum*)

IRIS (*Iris* Dutch hybrids)

IVY (*Hedera*)

JASMINE (*Jasminum*)
    Yellow jasmine (*Jasminum humile*)

JUNIPER (*Juniperus*)

KALE (*Brassica oleracea*)

KANGAROO PAW (*Anigozanthos*)

LADY'S MANTLE (*Alchemilla mollis*)

LADY'S SLIPPER (*Paphiopedilum*)

LAMB'S EAR (*Stachys byzantina*)

LARKSPUR (*Consolida ajacis*)

LEMON BALM (*Melissa officinalis*)

LILAC (*Syringa vulgaris*)
    'Primrose' (*Syringa vulgaris 'Primrose'*)
    'Sensation' (*Syringa vulgaris 'Sensation'*)

LILY GRASS (*Anthericum*)

LILY-OF-THE-VALLEY (*Convallaria majalis*)

LISIANTHUS (*Eustoma grandiflora*)

LOTUS FLOWER (*Lotus*)

LOVE-IN-A-MIST (*Nigella damascena*)

LUPINE / "BLUE BONNET" (*Lupinus*)

MADONNA LILY (*Lilium candidum*)

MAGNOLIA (*Magnolia*)

MAILE VINE (*Alyxia oliviformis*)

MARGUERITE DAISY (*Argyranthemum frutescens*)

MARIGOLD (*Tagetes*)

MOSS ON A STICK / INDIAN PON PON MUSK

MUSCARI / "GRAPE HYACINTH" (*Muscari*)
    Double muscari (*Muscari armeniacum 'Blue Spike'*)

NERINE LILY (*Nerine*)

NEW ZEALAND FLAX (*Phormium tenax*)

ORANGE BLOSSOM / "MEXICAN MOCK ORANGE" (*Philadelphus mexicanus*)

ORCHID (family Orchidaceae; orchid genera mentioned in the book appear below)
    Arachnis / "spider" orchid
    Cattleya
    Colmanara
    Cymbidium
    Dendrobium
        blush
        'Merry Mac'
    Epidendrum
    Mokara (not a genus, but a hybrid)
    Odontoglossum / "wildcat orchid"
    Oncidium
        'Sherry Baby'
    Paphiopedilum
    Phalaenopsis / "moth orchid" or "butterfly orchid"
    Vanda
    Zygopetalum

OREGANO (*Origanum*)

ORIENTAL LILY (*Lilium* hybrid cultivars, Oriental)
    'Broadway'
    'Casablanca'
    'Sumatra'
    'Xotica'

ORNAMENTAL PINEAPPLE / (*Ananas bracteatus 'Tricolor'*)

ORNITHOGALUM (*Ornithogalum*)
    Bumblebee (*Ornithogalum arabicum*)

OSCULARIA (*Oscularia deltoides*)

PAMPAS GRASS (*Cortaderia selloana*)

PANSY (*Viola*)

PAPERWHITE NARCISSUS (*Narcissus papyraceus*)
    'Erlicheer'

PAPYRUS (*Cyperus papyrus*)

PASSION FLOWER (*Passiflora*)

PEACH BLOSSOM (*Prunus persica*)

PEONY (*Paeonia*)
    "Tree Peony" (*Paeonia suffruticosa*)
    Dutch hybrids (*Paeonia lactiflora* cultivars)

PEPPERBERRY / "CALIFORNIAN (OR PERUVIAN) PEPPERBERRY" (*Shinus molle*)

PHILODENDRON (*Philodendron*)

PITTOSPORUM (*Pittosporum*)

PLUMERIA / "FRANGIPANI" (*Plumeria*)

PLUMOSA FERN (*Asparagus setaceus*)

PODOCARPUS (*Podocarpus*)

POPPY, BLUE HIMALAYAN (*Meconopsis simplicifolia*)

PRIVET (*Ligustrum japonicum*)

PROTEA (*Protea*)
    King (*Protea cynaroides*)
    Pincushion (*Leucospermum*)

PURPLE PINCUSHION (*Isopogon formosus*)

PURPLE VELVET (*Cacalia aurantiaca*)

PYRACANTHA (*Pyracantha*)

QUEEN ANNE'S LACE (*Daucus carota*)

RANUNCULUS (*Ranunculus*)

RATTLESNAKE GRASS (*Briza maxima*)

RHODODENDRON (*Rhododendron*)

ROSE (*Rosa*)
    'Akito'
    'Alabrahma'
    'Amsterdam'
    'Anushka'
    'Antique Romantica'
    'Aqua'
    'Avalanche'
    'Bianca Candy'
    'Big Fun'
    'Black Baccara'
    'Blue Curiosa'
    'Bluebird'
    'Bonfire'
    'Camel'
    'Carla Romantica'
    'Cherries Jubilee'
    'Cherry Brandy'
    'Circus'
    'Citronella'
    'Cool Water'
    'Coup Soleil'
    'Cortes Quatro'
    'Delilah'
    'Elektra'
    'Emanuelle'
    'Eric Taberly'
    'Esperance'
    'Evelyn'
    'First Lady'
    'Geisha'
    'Geneve'
    'Gertrude Jekyl'
    'Gypsy Curiosa'
    'Happy Hour'
    'Hocus Pocus'
    'Jade'
    'Juliette'
    'Juliette Drouet'
    'Karadise'

'Kirsche Royale'
'La Parisienne'
'Leah Romantica'
'Limona'
'Lollypop'
'Mari Romantica'
'Marie Claire'
'Marmalade'
'Marrakesh'
'Milva'
'Mimi Eden'
'Movie Star'
'Mystery'
'Naranja'
'Nightingale'
'Old Dutch'
'Pacific Blue'
'Pierre de Ronsard'
'Porcelina'
'Pullman Orient Express'
'Quatres Cortes'
'Ranuncula'
'Razzle Dazzle'
'Red Intuition'
'Revue'
'Riverdale'
'Rosita Vendela'
'Sahara'
'Sanaa'
'Sari'
'Shanty'
'Splendid Renate'
'Sterling Silver'
'Summer Fashion'
'Sunny Romantica'
'Super Green'
'Sweet Akito'
'Sweet Moments'
'Sweet Perfumela'
'Talea'
'Tenga Venga'
'Terra Cotta'
'Terranova'
'Valeria'
'Vendela'
'Yellow Island'
'Yves Piaget'

ROSEMARY (*Rosemarinus*)

SAGE (*Salvia officinalis*)

SANDERSONIA (*Sandersonia*)

SANTOLINA (*Santolina*)

SCABIOSA (*Scabiosa*)
    Blue lace (*Scabiosa caucasica*)
    Pincushion (*Scabiosa atropurpurea*)

SEA HOLLY (*Eryngium bourgatii*)

SILVER TREE (*Leucadendron argenteum*)

SMOKE BUSH (*Cotinus*)

SNAPDRAGON (*Antirrhinum*)

SNOWBERRY (*Symphoricarpos*)

SNOWDROP (*Gaultheria hispida*)

SPEARMINT (*Mentha spicata*)

SPIDER LILY (*Lycoris*)

STATICE (*Limonium sinuata*)

STEPHANOTIS (*Stephanotis floribunda*)

STOCK (*Matthiola incana*)

STRING OF BEADS (*Senecio rowleyanus*)

SUNFLOWER (*Helianthus*)

SWEET PEA (*Lathyrus odoratus*)

SWEET VIOLET (*Viola odorata*)

THYME (*Thymus*)

TI LEAF (*Cordyline fruticosa*)

TIGER LILY / "ASIATIC LILY" (*Tigrinum splendens*)

TOAD LILY (*Tricyrtis*)

TRACHELIUM (*Trachelium*)

TRUMPET LILY (*Lilium* hybrid cultivars, aurelian / "trumpet lily")
    'Triumphator'

TUBEROSE (*Polianthes tuberose*)

TULIP (*Tulipa*)
    Angelique (*Tulipa* hybrid cultivar Double Late 'Angelique')
    Parrot (*Tulipa* hybrid cultivars, Parrot Group)
    Weber's parrot (*Tulipa* hybrid cultivar Parrot Group 'Weber's Parrot')

TWEEDIA / "HEAVEN BOW" (*Tweedia caerulea* [a.k.a. *oxypetalum caeruleum*])

VERONICA (*Veronica*)

VIBURNUM (*Viburnum*)
    Guilder rose (*Viburnum opulus*)
    Snowball (*Viburnum plicatum*)
    Korean (*Viburnum carlesii*)

VIOLET (*Viola odorata*)

WAX FLOWER (*Chamelaucium*)

WHEAT (*Triticum*)

WINTERBUD / "SWEET HUCK" (*Vaccinium parvifolium*)

WINTER DAPHNE (*Daphne odora*)

YARROW (*Achillea*)

ZINNIA (*Zinnia*)

Resources

Tools, Florist, and Craft Supply

A. C. Moore
Arts and crafts supplies.
www.acmoore.com

Ben Franklin Crafts
Beading supplies.
www.benfranklincrafts.com

Filigree Monogram Designs
Custom monogrammed bouquet ribbon.
www.filigreemonograms.com

Hobby Lobby
Arts-and-crafts supplies.
www.hobbylobby.com

JoAnn Fabrics and Crafts
Indispensable resource for craft supplies.
www.joann.com

Michaels
Arts-and-crafts supplies.
www.michaels.com

Pacific Fabrics & Crafts
My favorite fabric store.
www.pacificfabrics.com

RomanticFlowers.com
Specialty florist supplies.
www.romanticflowers.com

Sears
Craftsman tools and toolboxes.
www.sears.com

Smith & Hawken
Flower pruners, gloves, and toolboxes.
www.smithandhawken.com

Other Resources

Bouquet preservation information:
Simone's Timeless Gardens. Seattle vicinity.
www.timelessgarden.com

Hollyhock Cakes. www.hollyhockcakes.com

For help finding a freeze-dry professional:
International Freeze-Dry Floral Association.
www.ifdfa.org

Information and classes on pressing flowers:
All About Pressed Flower Art, by Kate Chu.
www.pressed-flowers.info

For More Information

BOOKS

A Centennial History of the American Florist.
Topeka, KS: Florists' Review Enterprises,
1997.

Festive Flowers, by Paula Pryke. New York:
Rizzoli International, 2002.

*Flower Confidential: The Good, the Bad, and
the Beautiful in the Business of Flowers,* by Amy
Stewart. Chapel Hill, NC: Algonquin
Books, 2007.

Nature and Its Symbols, by Lucia Impelluso,
translated by Stephen Sartarelli. Los Angeles: J. P. Getty Museum, 2004.

WEB SITES

www.theflowerexpert.com
An online flowers encyclopedia.

www.flowercouncil.org
Flower Council of Holland.

www.brides.com
Brides can find local florists and other
vendors, see the latest wedding fashions,
register to create a wedding Web site, and
engage with other brides on community
newsgroups.

www.bouquetchic.com
For more information about this book and
the designs of Kimberly Aurora Kapur.

Credits

Cut flowers provided by:

AÑO NUEVO FLOWER GROWERS
Violet flower farmer to the trade.
Nationwide. 650-879-0389.

EUFLORIA FLOWERS
Specialty boutique roses to the trade.
Nationwide. 866-929-4683 in U.S.;
805-929-4683. www.eufloriaflowers.com

FLORABUNDANCE
Boutique wholesale flowers to the trade.
Nationwide. 800-201-3597.
www.florabundance.com

GARDEN VALLEY RANCH
Wholesale garden roses to the public and
the trade. Nationwide. 707-795-0919.
www.gardenvalley.com

NORTHWEST WHOLESALE FLORISTS
Wholesale to the public and the trade.
Seattle and vicinity. 206-622-5370.
www.nwwholesaleflorists.com

OREGON COASTAL FLOWERS
Wholesale specialty flowers to the public
and the trade. Nationwide. 503-815-3762.
www.flowersbulbs.com

TAYAMA GREENHOUSES, INC.
Wholesale specialty flowers and tropicals
to the trade. Los Angeles vicinity and
nationwide. 213-627-3473 (Los Angeles
location); 760-931-8038 (San Diego
location). www.tayama.com

Gowns provided by:

CICADA BRIDAL
Wedding gowns for customers in Seattle
and vicinity. 206-652-2434.
www.cicadabridal.com

LA BELLE ELAINE'S
Wedding gowns for customers in
Seattle and vicinity. 206-404-0888.
www.labelleelaines.com

LULY YANG COUTURE
Wedding gowns, groom's attire, maids'
dresses, and accessories for customers in
Seattle and vicinity. 206-623-8200.
www.lulyyang.com

SOMETHING BLUE BRIDAL
Wedding gowns for customers in LaConner,
Washington, and vicinity. 360-466-0415.
www.somethingblueboutique.com

VOLETTA COUTURE
Wedding gowns for customers in Bellevue,
Washington, and vicinity. 425-454-5020.
www.volettacouture.com

Featured North American Gown Designers

AMY KUSCHEL
415-956-5657. www.amykuschel.com

ANNE BARGE
404-873-8070. www.annebarge.com

AVIOANNI
416-585-2611. www.avioanni.com

BADGLEY MISCHKA
310-248-3750. www.badgleymischka.com

CARMELA SUTERA
973-471-7444. www.carmelasutera.com

ELIZABETH FILLMORE
212-647-0863.
www.elizabethfillmorebridal.com

INES DI SANTO
866-899-ines. www.inesdisanto.com

KATHRYN AND ALEXANDRA
800-356-3739.
www.kathrynandalexandra.com

LULY YANG COUTURE
206-623-8200. www.lulyyang.com

MADINA VADACHE
206-985-8967. www.madinavadache.com

NICOLE MILLER
888-300-6258. www.nicolemiller.com

RICHARD GLASGOW
Available through La Belle Elaine's
www.labelleelaines.com

SAISON BLANCHE
877-272-4766. www.saisonblanche.com

SALLY CREW
Available through La Belle Elaine's.
www.labelleelaines.com.

VERA WANG
212-628-3400. wwww.verawang.com

Featured European Gown Designers

ELIE SAAB
(+34) 900-100-075; in U.S: 516-872-5710.
www.pronovias.com

ENMANUEL COUTURE
866-776-7238. www.enmanuelcouture.com

JENNY PACKHAM
(+44) 0-20-7267-1864.
www.jennypackhambride.com

PRONOVIAS
(+34) 900-100-075; in U.S: 516-872-5710.
www.pronovias.com

LE SPOSA DI GIÒ
(+34) 900-100-075; in U.S: 516-872-5710.
www.pronovias.com

VALENTINO
(+34) 900-100-075; in U.S: 516-872-5710.
www.pronovias.com/valentino

Accessories and shoes provided by:

ANNE KLEIN shawl from Macy's.
www.macys.com

BELLA UMBRELLA.
Nationwide vintage umbrella rentals.
www.bellaumbrella.com

DONNA KARAN AND JOEY O shoes
from Zappos. www.zappos.com

CASSINI FUR BOLERO through La Belle
Elaine's. www.labelleelaines.com

EMITATIONS
www.emitations.

INGE CHRISTOPHER handbags
from Zappos. www.zappos.com

KRISTEN ELIZABETH VEILS. Nationwide.
603-778-6440. www.kristenelizabeth.com.

LULY YANG private collection accessories
and shoes. www.lulyyang.com

MICHAL NEGRIN jewelry from Romantic-
Flowers. www.romanticflowers.com

NADRI, CARA COUTURE ACCESSORIES,
AND BETSEY JOHNSON accessories available from Nordstrom. www.nordstrom.com

RODO shoes (www.rodo.it)
available through Luly Yang Couture.
www.lulyyang.com

SAKS FIFTH AVENUE
www.saksfifthavenue.com

SISTERS ANTIQUES
www.sistersantiques.com

TWO'S COMPANY accessories from
www.romanticflowers.com.

Ribbons and trimmings provided by:

RomanticFlowers AND
RomanticRibbons (unless otherwise
noted below): retail sales of ribbons, trims
and florist supplies. www.romanticflowers.
com and www.romanticribbons.com

APPLIQUÉ TRIM for "Eydie" bouquet
(page 54) by Roth International,
available at Pacific Fabrics & Crafts.
www.pacificfabrics.com

RICKRACK for "Betsy" bouquet
(page 127) by Wrights Trims.

Furnishings and props provided by:

MAISON DE FRANCE
Bellevue, Washington. French furnishings,
linens, dinnerware, flatware, bridal registry.
425-688-1078. www.maisondefrance.com

SISTERS ANTIQUES
Issaquah, Washington. Unique vintage
pieces for the home. 425-392-7373.
www.sistersantiques.com

TWO ANGELS ANTIQUES
Seattle, Washington. Classical European
antique furnishings. 206-340-6005.
www.twoangelsantiques.com

Photographs in this book were shot at these locations:

Bellevue Botanical Gardens. Bellevue,
Washington. www.bellevuebotanical.org

Daylight Studios. Seattle, Washington.
www.daylightstudioseattle.com

Maison de France. Bellevue, Washington.
www.maisondefrance.com

Pensione Nichols Bed & Breakfast. Seattle,
Washington. www.pensionenichols.com

Two Angels Antiques, Seattle, Washington.
www.twoangelsantiques.com

Index